THE GOOD, THE BAD,
and
THE SAVED

Larry Clements

ISBN 978-1-64114-749-1 (paperback)
ISBN 978-1-64114-750-7 (digital)

Christian Faith Publishing, Inc.
832 Park Avenue
Meadville, PA 16335
www.christianfaithpublishing.com

Printed in the United States of America

TABLE OF CONTENTS

Introduction

THIS BOOK IS A SHORT story of my life. It talks about where I was, where I'm at, and where I am going. It is a book about life and death. It's about the choices we make and the consequences of them.

It's not a crime story, but there is a lot of it mentioned. Divorce and drugs are talked about as well, but it isn't a book about either of those. It isn't a book on religion; yet without God, I could not, or would not have written it. The purpose of writing it is to hopefully get you thinking about eternity.

We all make choices in life, some good and some bad. But there is one decision we all need to make in our life, and that is will we choose life or death.

As you read this book, I'm sure there will be a lot of you that can relate to it in one way or another; some will just reject it flat out. That's OK. I don't agree with everyone either. It isn't to get you to agree with me. It's just me telling my story and my experience. Hopefully, you can glean some good out of it.

If this book will help one person to come to know God and the love He has for them, then it was all worth it.

CHAPTER ONE

Young and Dumb

In the beginning, I suppose I wasn't such a bad kid. But that was from my mom's perspective. Parents don't want to acknowledge that their kids are bad, especially moms, but having an understanding of what the Bible teaches on the matter helps us understand why even good kids do bad things.

The Bible tells us that in the beginning, God made everything, and "it was very good" (Genesis 1:31). It wasn't until sin entered the world that things started to go bad. "Therefore, just as through one man sin entered the world, and death through sin, and thus death spread to all men, because all sinned" (Romans 5:12).

In other words, the first man and woman God created sinned against Him simply by eating a piece of fruit that He told them not to eat. That was when man became a sinner and sin entered into the world. God did not create the sin, but man made it, if you will. With that being said, every man and woman from that point on was born into sin. That is why a good kid can do bad things, because he has a sin nature passed down from Adam and Eve.

It reminds me of this story I once heard. This guy had been out shopping for groceries before he came home and began putting things away in the kitchen cabinets. His son, who was about four or five years old at the time, saw him putting away some candy in a drawer. The boy asked his dad, "Can I have some candy?" The father said, "Not now; we're going to be eating dinner soon." The dad then made it clear to his son not to get into the candy. The son replied, "OK, Dad!"

The father went to tend to other business in the house, but as time passed by, the father hadn't heard a peep from his son. The father became concerned about his whereabouts. Going through the house searching for his son, he entered into the kitchen. There was his son, with chocolate all over his face. Busted! He asked, "Have you been eating the candy I told you not to eat?" The boy answered with an emphatic, "No Dad!"

The boy thought he had gotten away with eating it because when his dad came into the kitchen, the candy had already been eaten. The evidence was gone! Or so the boy thought. It's kind of funny, yet it proves the point that even a little boy or girl has a sin nature.

Do you suppose that father taught that young boy to lie? I would hope not. I don't think any good parent would. No one had to teach that boy to lie; it came naturally. That illustration, for me, confirms what the Bible teaches about us all being born into sin. "The wicked are estranged from the womb; they go astray as soon as they are born, speaking lies" (Psalm 58:3). Even a little boy or girl, no matter how innocent they may seem, is born into sin. This is so important to know and understand as we continue to learn more about the meaning of life and death.

As for me not being such a bad kid, well, my father had a different perspective from that of my mother's. My dad was a strict father, which I attribute to him being a military career man spending twenty years in the navy.

He was a World War II veteran who served on the aircraft carrier USS *Yorktown*. He was aboard that ship during the Battle of Midway when the Japanese sank it.

Pops was a hard worker and provided for my mom and his five kids. He had a lot of good qualities. It's unfortunate it seems I can only remember the bad ones—or should I say, bad habits. My dad was an alcoholic during my childhood days, and it wasn't until his later years in life that he did quit drinking.

He wasn't one to express much of his feelings or emotions. I never heard him say, "I love you" to any of us kids or my mom. I'm sure he did, but I never felt it or heard it expressed in words.

Mostly what I felt and heard from him was anger and displeasure in three of the four boys. We were always told we were worthless and weren't going to amount to anything. I can only speak for myself, but if I didn't do well in school, I usually got a belt whipping.

I can remember one time when I was in the seventh or eighth grade. The students were entrusted to carry their report card home with them to show their parents. They ended up changing that policy due to some untrustworthy students—me being one of them. They started mailing them home *and that was all bad for me.*

Before, when the teacher gave me my report card to take home, I would change the grades on it before I got to my house. Back in my day, the report cards were handwritten. Since they weren't typed, it was really easy to change an F into a B. The hardest part was to match the ink color.

I came home from school one day, and that was the day my report card landed at the house. As soon as I walked in the door, my dad said to me, "Call all of your friends. We're having a party." To say the least, I knew something was wrong. My dad hated my friends, and I knew he was up to something.

It totally slipped my mind about the report cards being mailed out. At that point in time, he hadn't showed me the report card. I responded, "They can't come!" Again he told me to call them. *Now I'm really starting to panic.* I told him, "They can't come!" He said, "Call your friends. We're having a party, an ass-kicking party, and you're the one supplying the ass." That was when he showed me the report card. I had four Fs and a D-. Needless to say, I wasn't excelling in school.

He told me to get my PJs on and started to take his belt off. He proceeded to whip me and whip me and whip me. If it were not for my older brother Bruce stepping in and saying that was enough, who knew how long I would have gotten whipped.

Growing up, I had a lot of resentment toward my dad for the way he physically treated me. That was his form of correction, a belt whipping. Today I think they would call it child abuse. I really don't blame him for being angry with me. After all, what parent wouldn't be angry with his kid for getting four Fs and a D-?

Kids should be disciplined, but I think there is difference between discipline and punishment. Correcting a child because of the love you have for them, that's great discipline. But when you react in anger to a child misbehaving, then I believe that's misdirected punishment.

A friend once said; "When it came to disciplining my children, I would say to them; go to your room and think about what you just did. In five minutes I'll come in and we'll discuss what we are going to do about your behavior. He said the five minutes gave the kid's time to think about what Dad was going to do to them, but more important, it gave him five minutes to calm down and not punish them in anger" (Don Emmons). I think that is the best advice ever.

There is a scripture in the book of Hebrews that made me realize that my dad raised us kids the best he knew how. We learn traits from our parents, and I'm sure my dad raised us the same way his dad raised him—with an iron fist!

The Bible talks about how God chastens those He loves. In the same text, it talks about how human fathers correct their children. In Hebrews 12:10, it says, "For they [human fathers] indeed for a few days chastened us as seemed best to them, but He [God, the Father] for our profit, that we may be partakers of His holiness."

That one verse in the Bible allowed me not only to forgive my dad for the physical abuse but also to understand that he did the best he knew how. Just as our parents want us to do good, well, God wants the same thing. That's why parents and God correct those whom they love.

My dad passed away on August 5, 2012, due to aspirating in his sleep and complications from pneumonia. My brother Ron and I were both at the hospital when Dad passed away. It was quite an experience to watch my dad take his last breath. *One minute, you have life; the next, you don't.*

CHAPTER TWO

When the Spirit Leaves

To SEE MY DAD DIE was heartbreaking and caused many sleepless nights afterward. I guess it's because I'm not sure where he is today. Oh, his body is in the grave, but where did his spirit go? Two things are very real: life and death.

The Bible speaks about when you die and how your spirit leaves your body. Either it goes to be with the Lord in heaven, if you believe in Jesus Christ as Lord and Savior, or it goes to Hades, where those who haven't repented and placed their trust in Jesus Christ as their Lord and Savior are.

It became evident to me that this is true. The moment my dad took his last breath, he immediately became white as a ghost. *His spirit had left his body at that very instant.* What an eye-opening experience. I had no clue it was so abrupt. It was literally just a matter of a second or two before he turned white as a ghost.

I just mentioned Heaven and Hades; whether we believe in heaven and hell or not doesn't change the fact they are both real. Where did my dad's spirit go? Only God and my dad know the answer to that question for sure. But the Bible does talk about a *second death—not just in the physical sense, but also in the Spiritual.*

God didn't create hell for you or me. He created it for the devil and his angels. However, if you want to follow Satan, he'll be there in hell waiting for you. That's as real as it gets.

You might be saying, "I don't follow Satan!" maybe not knowingly, but remember that little boy with the candy and how he lied to his dad? Here is a couple of verses in scripture that I hope will clarify it for you: "He who overcomes shall inherit all things, and I will be his God and he shall be My son. But the cowardly, unbelieving, abominable, murderers, sexually immoral, sorcerers, idolaters, and all *liars* shall have their part in the lake which burns with fire and brimstone, which is the *second death*" (Revelation 21:7–8, emphasis added). Did that little boy lie? I'm not saying that little boy is going to the lake of fire; I'm saying even that little boy needs to be saved from that lake of fire. *Jesus Christ is that Savior.* Jesus died for his, mine, and your sins.

I remember this one time when I was a kid. I was sent to my room for talking while my dad was trying to watch TV. I wasn't much older than the boy who lied about eating the candy. I was crying, mad and wanted to watch TV too!

While in my room, I got a brainstorm; I jumped out of the window and walked down to the corner drugstore. I ended up in the candy section. *So what is it with the candy and little boys?* I can't remember what I picked out, but I do remember I didn't have any money to buy it. I then shoved the candy into my pocket and left the store. When I got home to eat my candy, I found it wasn't so bad to be in my room after all. It was about that time when my dad yelled out, "You can come out of your room now!" I was a happy camper! I got to eat candy and now watch TV. It didn't get any better than that.

Now I'm thinking it pays to sin. I wasn't thinking about the sin; I was just thinking about how happy I was now. By the way, it does pay to sin; I just don't think you'll like the wages. "For the wages of sin is death, but the gift of God is eternal life in Christ Jesus our Lord" (Romans 6:23). God is going to demand payment for our sins, and the payment is death. But (I love that word), *but* we have eternal life in Christ Jesus, our Lord.

Jesus made the payment that was due. He took the sins of the world upon Himself and nailed them to the cross. That's where God the Father poured out His judgment on Jesus, His Son, for our sins. They weren't Jesus's sins; they were ours! Jesus died for us so that we may have life.

There is a story in the Bible that talks about death, life, and the power Jesus has over death. This woman, Martha, had a brother who died and was dead for four days. Jesus came on the scene, and Martha said to Jesus, "Lord, if You had been here, my brother would not have died." Further along in the story, Jesus said to Martha, "I am the resurrection and the life. He who believes in Me, though he may die, he shall live. And whoever lives and believes in Me shall never die. Do you believe this?' (John 11:21, 25–26).

Jesus is asking you right now, do you believe what He told Martha? If you are wondering if Jesus raised Martha's brother Lazarus from the dead, He did! The story is in the book of John 11:1–44. I would encourage you to read it.

If you don't believe in life after death, that's OK. I didn't believe the entire Word of God either. But if you think there might be something to it, then it would be to your benefit to continue to read on. One thing is obvious: death is real. The question is, Is there life after death? And if there is, do you want it? I pray that you do.

CHAPTER THREE

Know-It-All

In my teenager years, I knew it all. Maybe you know a teenager like that? Maybe you are that teenager. Speaking for myself, no one could tell me anything! I knew everything there was to know about life. *I had no clue.* I just thought I knew. The truth of the matter is, *I was lost.* The life I was living was one leading to death.

At a young age of thirteen or fourteen, I wanted to join the Boy Scouts. Two of my friends were in the club, and it was something I wanted to do. I asked my mom if I could join. Of course I got the, "Ask your dad if you can" response. I did, and it wasn't the answer I wanted. His answer was, "I'm not going to spend a bunch of money on uniforms, etc." It wasn't a happy moment in my life.

Since I couldn't join the Boy Scouts and hang out with my friends, what was I going to do now? I decided to go out and find some new friends. They weren't the kind you want to bring home to Mom. I think you know what I mean.

I started smoking pot with my new friends. The high I got from this drug took my mind off of wanting to be a Boy Scout. Now all I wanted to do was get high. I didn't realize where this was going to take me in life, but at the time I thought it was cool. *It was a lie and I fell for it.*

A Christian friend, Henry Alviso, once told me, "If you don't know the truth, you'll fall for the lie." I replaced the truth for a lie. The truth was, I wanted to do something good. I wanted to become a Boy Scout! When I couldn't, I believed the lie would make me feel better. I didn't feel any better getting loaded, it just made me forget the hurt I had of not being able to join the Boy Scouts.

Falling for the lie just put me into bondage. Being under the influence of a drug or alcohol is bondage. It will control your actions and the decisions you make in life. If you don't think so, you've already fallen for the lie! The thing is, everyone is controlled by someone or something.

Everyone wants to feel in control of their life. When I was getting high, I felt in control. When I wasn't loaded, my dad had the control. He chose what I did or didn't do. Being under the influence of a drug is just that; you are being influenced by the drug. *It is, in all actuality, controlling you.*

I want God to be the influence in my life. I know it won't be a perfect life, but without His word and His Spirit, I know I would be a total wreck. The book of Romans touches on what I just said about everyone being controlled by someone or something: "Do you not know that to whom you present yourselves slaves to obey, you are that one's slaves whom you obey, whether of sin leading to death, or of obedience leading to righteousness" (Romans 6:16). So if you're practicing sin, you're a slave to it. If you're practicing obedience to God's Word, then you're a slave of righteousness. I guess my question would be, what is controlling you, and whom are you a slave to?

I was a slave to the devil and I did what the devil does, evil things. In no way am I proud of the things I've done, but I do want people to know God has delivered me from them. If you're in a similar situation, He can deliver you too! God can and does deliver those who ask Him. That is why Jesus came into the world, to save us from the penalty of sin. And as you just read, that penalty is death.

About the same time I started hanging out with my newfound friends, my oldest brother, Robert, was arrested for murder and armed robbery. I always wanted to be like my older brother, and now I had a template to follow.

My thinking changed from wanting to be a Boy Scout, to that of being a gangster. His arrest helped validate who I wanted to be: a gangster!

Hanging out with the wrong people will affect the way you think and live. Hanging around Boy Scouts, I wanted to be one. Hanging around drug users and thieves, I wanted to be one.

Young kids are easily influenced and should choose the right friends. Parents should help in that process of finding good friends for their children. "The righteous should choose his friends carefully, For the way of the wicked leads them astray" (Proverbs 12:26). There are so many verses in the Bible about whom someone should or shouldn't associate with.

My dad started to say about my *new* friends, "They're going to get you into trouble!" What he failed to realize was, I had good friends doing good things. I felt the need to have new friends because I didn't have a Boy Scout uniform. I don't know if he ever did realize the mistake he made by not letting me join the Boy Scouts. I know I never did tell him.

Young boys are full of energy and want something to do. If they're not led in the right direction, then chances are, they will choose the wrong path in life. That's probably why the Bible says for parents to, "Train up a child in the way he should go, and when he is old he will not depart from it" (Proverbs 22:6).

On top of hanging around with friends that were into drugs and an older brother that I wanted to be like, I started to watch gangster movies on TV. Movies like Dillinger, Pretty Boy Floyd, Al Capone, Bonnie and Clyde, etc.

TV had a big influence on me while I was growing up. I'm not saying TV is bad; I'm saying it can and does have an influence on young kids. I would say adults aren't excluded from that influence as well.

As parents, we should be cautious of what our kids watch on TV. Kids are obviously going to watch some TV in their lifetime. When they do, watch it with them. If you don't, at least know what the content is of what they are watching.

It played a big role in the way I lived my life and left a long-lasting impression on me. I had that gangster mentality for most of my life, and I can honestly say that TV played a big part in that. I can't single TV out as the culprit to my demise, but it definitely played its part.

As a teenager, I was in and out of juvenile hall. There are too many times to count or list, but I'll mention a couple of them. My high school principal, Mr. Kaufman, filed truancy charges against me and I ended up spending a couple of weeks in juvenile hall for that. I didn't need to go to school! Remember, *I already knew everything.*

At the age of sixteen, my friend and I robbed a 7-Eleven with a .22-caliber rifle. This was one of my *new* friends, by the way. We got busted about twenty minutes later, and I spent six months in a juvenile camp.

It was a crazy lifestyle, and I loved it. I can remember eating reds like they were candy. For those of you that don't know what reds are, they were pills that would get you so loaded, it was like having too much to drink. We used to call them fender benders. That was because when you ate them and drove a car, you usually wrecked the car and bent a fender, at the least. I wrecked a lot of cars in my *"I know it all"* years.

At the age of sixteen I worked for a place called Me-N-Ed's Pizza. I was scheduled to work on New Year's Eve, which wasn't a problem until I ate some reds before going to work. Prior to that day, I had put in for a transfer to work at another pizza parlor. I was waiting for that transfer to come through when I went to work that night. Now being under the influence of the reds, I decided I no longer wanted to work on New Year's. I wanted to go party with my friends.

I told the manager I couldn't work that night. I don't remember what reason I gave him, but I'm sure he knew it was because I was loaded. He said, "If you don't work tonight, you're not getting your transfer." Not happy with his reply, I pulled a switchblade out of my front pocket which I just bought the weekend before in Tijuana. This was my new toy, and I figured I'd try it out on my boss.

I don't recall what I said to him at that point, but I'm sure it wasn't anything nice. I was too loaded to remember what I said. I do remember that a guy grabbed me from behind and put me in a bear hug.

My first reaction was to try to stab this guy in his leg with the knife so he would let me go. Meanwhile, this other guy picked up a metal stirring paddle that we used to mix dough with. He then began hitting me over the top of my hand with this metal paddle to knock the knife out.

It wasn't like what you see in the movies, where after the first hit the knife flies out of the hand. It took several hits, and it wasn't the actual hit that knocked it out. It was because it hurt like heck every time he hit me, and I just didn't want to get hit anymore. My coworkers retrieved the knife, and then the one holding me let go. I ran out into the parking lot and jumped into my dad's car and took off.

This was a classic 1956 Plymouth, which Pops would let me use to drive back and forth to work. He bought this car from an older guy named Charlie who was the original owner. I couldn't believe how well Charlie had maintained this car. *This was a cherry car.* I know my dad was proud of it.

After I left the pizza parlor, I was driving home on the freeway when I came to my exit. The exit turned to the right, but I didn't. I crashed into the guardrail, taking out the left front side of my dad's car. Fender bender! Now I was afraid to go home. I knew I was going to get one of those report card parties that I wasn't really fond of. So I did what any brave wannabe gangster would do. *I called my mom.*

"Ma, I crashed Clem's car, and the police are looking for me for pulling a knife on my boss. I'm not coming home, because I know Clem [that's what we used to call my dad]. He will kill me, and I know the police are going to arrest me." My mom reassured me that if I came home now my dad wouldn't whip me. That was due to the fact they had close friends over at the house visiting, and now would be the best time for me to come home.

Thank God their friends were still there when I got home. I don't know how I got out of a beating and being arrested, but I escaped them both. My boss fired me obviously, but he didn't press charges. My dad apparently had talked to him and persuaded him not to press charges. The wrecked car was another story. It never was the same.

At the time, I didn't think anything of it. I just knew I got out of a whole lot of trouble. I avoided a whipping from my dad and going to juvenile hall. As far as I was concerned, it was no big deal. I had fun getting loaded and didn't get into trouble for it.

It was a big deal, and sin does have consequences. I didn't see it then, but everyone involved that night was impacted. The impact it had on me was the loss of my job. My boss and coworkers were traumatized by the whole ordeal. My dad's car got wrecked. My mother was worried to death about her son.

Here I was, thinking I got away with something. I really didn't! God knows every sin, every thought, and every hair that is on our heads. Remember what the cost is for our sins: "For the wages of sin is death" (Romans 6:23). *I wasn't getting away with anything; I just thought I was.*

CHAPTER FOUR

Armed and Loaded

ONE OF MY PREVIOUS ARRESTS was for robbing a 7-Eleven store clerk. When my crime partner and I robbed the store, we were both under the influence of reds. It is one thing robbing a store armed with a loaded gun, but it's another story when the person robbing the store is loaded on reds.

Most of the bad things I've done in life were because I was drunk or loaded. I say *most*, only because there were occasions when I did do bad things when I wasn't high. For instance, there were times I would rob, steal, cheat, or lie to someone for the sole purpose of hustling them out of their money. It was all for the sake of obtaining drugs or alcohol for myself. The bottom line is, whether I was drunk, loaded, or not loaded, I am a sinner and was a slave to it.

While I was doing time at Joplin Boys Ranch in Southern California for that armed robbery is when I first heard about Jesus. The director of the boys ranch was Mr. Stripe. He was not only the director of the boy's camp, but he was also the pastor of a local church down the road. He is a very honorable man and has since gone to be with the Lord in heaven.

Mr. Stripe was the man who decided when a boy doing time at the camp was ready to be released from custody and go home. With that being said, he was the guy you wanted to look good in front of. When Sunday morning came around and it was church call, you definitely wanted to attend—only because Mr. Stripe was the pastor and he was your ticket home.

I guess you could say I went to church under false pretenses. But I do believe God used that situation in my life to plant a seed of belief in my heart. I think it was from that point on in my life that I would always say, "I believe in Jesus." But in all actuality, I still lived like the devil.

The demons believe in Jesus, but are they saved? "You believe that there is one God. You do well. Even the demons believe and tremble" (James 2:19). They believed Jesus was the Son of God, but they weren't saved. Why?

There is a story in the gospel of Matthew that will clarify it. "When He [Jesus] had come to the other side [of a lake] to the country of the Gergesenes, there met Him two demon-possessed men, coming out of the tombs, exceedingly fierce, so that no one could pass that way. And suddenly they cried out, saying, *what have we to do with You*, Jesus, You Son of God? Have You come to torment us before our time?" (Matthew 8:28–29, emphasis added).

The demon-possessed men believed Jesus to be the Son of God but replied, *"What have we to do with you?"* They *believed* but wanted nothing to do with Him. Some people don't want anything to do with Jesus, only because they're afraid they may have to give up their sin. *I know I didn't want to give mine up.* But you know what I found out? Once I gave my life to Jesus, I didn't have to give up anything. God replaced my sinful way of living with works of righteousness. *He wants to do the same for you.*

I can tell you from experience that it is a heck of a lot easier to be a slave of righteousness than it is to be a slave of the devil. Don't get me wrong, you'll still have trouble in your life; but with God in control of things, they end up working out for good. "And we know that all things work together for good to those who love God, to those who are the called according to His purpose" (Romans 8:28).

Some things in life aren't going to be so good, but some will. The Bible teaches that if you love God, it is then His promise to *work out all things for good.* That is a promise from God you can count on. He has not lied to me yet, nor will He.

All the bad things that I have created for myself in life, God is now working out for good. By sharing my past with someone who may actually be living the same type of life I once lived, I can say to you that no matter how bad you are, or even how good you think you are, Jesus loves you and died for you. *He wants to give you life and life more abundant.*

CHAPTER FIVE

None the Wiser

THEY SAY YOU'RE AN ADULT at the age of eighteen, but I would beg to differ. It was at that age I petitioned the courts to have my juvenile record sealed. It was a lengthy process, but it was granted, and my record was sealed. I had a brand-new start at life and *I just knew* things were going to be different. Now I was an adult with a clean record. It was *just as if I had never sinned*. You could actually substitute that last sentence with one word: *justified* (*just-if-ied* never sinned).

The Bible talks about how man is justified by faith in Christ Jesus. It's by placing your faith in Jesus Christ as your Lord and Savior. *It is just if you had never sinned*. Your sins are forgiven, and God remembers them no more. It isn't that He can't remember them; it's because He chooses not to remember. Ultimately, this is whom we need to be justified by: God.

I don't know about you, but there is always someone bringing up my past. Maybe your past isn't as dark as mine. If you've ever done someone wrong or hurt them in some way, they're usually there to remind you of it. God isn't like that. He will never bring up your sins again.

Micah, a prophet of God, speaks about what God will do with our sins: "He will again have compassion on us, and will subdue our iniquities. You will cast all our sins into the depths of the sea" (Micah

7:19). Our sins will be cast into the sea, and I thank God for that, because the new start in life I just mentioned, it didn't begin very well.

It was also at the age of eighteen I was given a traffic citation for driving on the wrong side of the road. Actually, the officer was being pretty cool in only giving me a ticket since I was loaded out of my mind on reds. Of course, I provoked him into including a citation for bald tires. When I was high on reds, I was an idiot. By all rights he should have taken me to jail, and I really wish he had.

My first wife, Cindy, was with me at the time this happened. I know it was only because of her charm that the officer let me go with just a ticket. He even told me, "If it wasn't for your wife, you'd be gone for being under the influence." He instructed her to drive from that point on.

As the officer was writing the ticket, I was taunting him to go ahead and write it. What I wasn't telling him was that I would get even later. I didn't know what I was going to do, but I knew I was going to do something.

Later on throughout that same day, I started to tell everyone I was going to firebomb the police station tonight. Most of the responses I received were, "Oh yeah," "Sure you are," "Quit joking around," etc. As the day wore on, I had totally forgotten all about the firebombing idea. That was only because I continued to eat reds and drink beer all day. Isn't it amazing how drugs and alcohol will diminish your ability to remember? *No duh.*

After hanging out with my wife's brothers and friends all day, my wife and I left for home. It was about 10:00 P.M. when we got there. I asked my wife to make me something to eat. Let me rephrase that; I told my wife to make me something to eat. She said, "No! You'll pass out by the time the food is done, so I'm not making it." I got mad and left to go to Jack in the Box.

When I got into the car, still drunk and loaded, I noticed a soda bottle on the floorboard. That soda bottle reminded me of the mission I had talked so much about during the day: *firebomb the police station.* All of a sudden, I was not hungry but searching for a gas station to put gas into this bottle to make a firebomb.

Back in 1975, gas stations closed at 9:00 or 10:00 PM, so I had to search for an open one. That was how determined I was to accomplish what I set out to do. I finally found one and pulled up to the pumps. I filled the bottle up and shoved a rag in the top of it. From there, I proceeded to drive to the Garden Grove Police Station.

I backed into someone's driveway across the street from the police station. I was trying to be inconspicuous. I didn't want a cop pulling out of the back of the police station to see me parked at their entrance. That would have been a definite roust. Back then, they didn't have cameras everywhere like they do today. So I wasn't worried about that.

There were two entrances to the back of the police station where the cops parked their vehicles. The west side entrance is the fire station; which is actually adjoined to the Police Department. That was the side I came in from. I wanted to come in from that side because that was where the gas pumps are. All police and emergency vehicles filled up there. I thought to myself, *This is my target, the gas pumps.*

I had never done anything like this before, and making a firebomb wasn't on my résumé. I wanted to take precautions so this thing wouldn't blow up in my hand. I figured if I had my arm cocked back in a throwing position, lit the rag, and tossed it as fast as possible, I'd be OK. Keep in mind the rag was just stuffed in the top of the bottle. There was nothing securing the rag to the bottle or preventing it from igniting the fuel inside. I lit the rag and threw it at the gas pumps. I took off running when I turned around to watch it explode. To my amazement and dissatisfaction, the rag was sitting there burning on the ground. I was disappointed but still determined.

I ran back to my car and drove to the first store I saw open. I bought a soda and dumped it out on the ground outside. I jumped back in my car and drove to the gas station where I had purchased the first bottle of gas. I think the attendant thought I was crazy. *I think he was right.*

I went back to the same street where I had parked earlier. I was going to back into the same driveway to throw this second firebomb at the same target. I didn't stand a chance; cops were crawling all over the place. Later on at my court hearing, I found out that someone in the fire station heard the bottle break and went out to investigate. The police were on full alert by the time I came back for more.

The cops observed me driving down the street to where the west entrance of the police station was. I knew they were on to me, so I started to leave the scene. A patrol car got in behind me and started to follow. Unknowingly I made a turn onto a dead-end street. That was when I had a brainstorm to throw the firebomb out the passenger window. I did that as I was turning around at the end of the street. I didn't think he would see me throw it as I turned. *He did.* He hit his red lights and pulled me over.

With guns drawn, and now half the police force there, I was ordered out of the car. I stepped back to the hood of the officer's car when he said, "Take everything out of your pockets and put it on the hood of the car." I reached in my front pocket and forgot all about having a half ounce of weed in there. I didn't take it out but proceeded to make sure everything else was out of my other pockets. Then I went back to the front pocket where the weed was, as if I was checking to make sure I got everything out. I then cupped the half ounce of weed in my left hand and made a fist with both hands and placed them on the hood of the car. The officer patted me down and didn't find the pot in my hands. Then I was placed into the back of his patrol car. That was when I took the weed and stashed it in his back seat, never to be found-at least not that night.

I had actually learned that trick from a previous arrest by the Garden Grove police. They were placing me in a holding cell at the police station when I realized I had a few reds in my pocket. The officer instructed me in the same way: "Take everything out of your pockets." I cupped the pills in my hand and placed the closed fists on the wall as he proceeded to pat me down, not checking my hands. He went out of the cell and shut the door. I then popped the pills in my mouth and got even higher than I was when I got busted, *thinking all along I got away with another one.* Sometimes I think that's why I continued in the lifestyle I was living. I kept thinking I was slick and was getting away with something.

Because my juvenile record had been sealed, it appeared as though this firebomb incident was my first arrest. After plea-bargaining, I received sixty days in jail and three years' probation for the firebombing attempt.

It sounds crazy, but in a way, I think the district attorney knew exactly what he was doing. He knew that if I continued in that type of lifestyle, the probation would end up being my downfall. It was, and I ended up going back to jail several times on probation violations. After two years of being on probation, the system finally got tired of me breaking the law and probation stipulations. They sentenced me to, (one to five years) in state prison for a probation violation. That was the first of my five terms in prison.

CHAPTER SIX

Insight

SINCE COMING TO THE TRUTH of who Jesus is and asking Him for guidance in my life, I now realize the reason I continued in the lifestyle I was living was not because I got away with so much; it was because I had a sin nature and it was the natural thing to do. *People apart from God do bad things.*

Scripture talks about how people are dead because of sin but how God, through faith in Jesus Christ, has made us alive. I'd like to share with you three verses from the book of Ephesians 2:1–3: "And you He made alive, who were dead in trespasses and sins, in which you once walked according to the course of this world, according to the prince of the power of the air [which is Satan], the spirit who now works in the sons of disobedience, among whom also we all once conducted ourselves in the lusts of our flesh, fulfilling the desires of the flesh and of the mind, and were by nature children of wrath, just as the others."

Notice how it says, "We *all once* conducted ourselves"? Prior to a person giving their life to God, we *all* are children of wrath and *sons of disobedience.* That's why I did bad things, because I was a child of wrath and not of God. I was a slave to sin and didn't even know it.

Some may say we are all children of God. This is true to some degree. Life does come from God, whether physical or spiritual. As physical beings, we are born into this world. The bad news is, the world is under the sway of Satan.

In a letter written by the apostle Paul to the Corinthian church, he says, "But even if our gospel [*gospel* means "good news"] is veiled to those who are perishing, whose minds the god of this age has blinded who do not believe, lest the light of the gospel of the glory of Christ, who is the image of God, should shine on them" (2 Corinthians 4:3–4).

Satan is referred to as the god of this age. He has blinded those who do not believe in God. Blinded them from what? The truth! Jesus says, "I am the way, the truth and the life. No one comes to the Father except through Me" (John 14:6).

Satan is a liar and the father of lies and doesn't want you to know you're his slave. That's how he keeps you in bondage to sin, by blinding you from the truth. The truth is that we are all sinners and need to be saved from the death sentence that sin brings.

As I previously mentioned, "if you don't know the truth, you'll fall for the lie" (Henry Alviso). That statement is so true. I fell for the lie most of my life, and it cost me years of my freedom. Now at the age of sixty-one, I have approximately twenty years in youth and adult prisons, only because I believed the lie.

Learning the truth has not only set me free from the spiritual imprisonment Satan had me in, but I have been delivered out of physical prison as well. It's only by God's grace that my last prison sentence was *only* thirteen years. The reason I say *only* is because I was facing eighty years to life. That's like a drop in the bucket compared to life.

After I had served a little over five years of that thirteen-year sentence was when the Lord Jesus got my attention. That was when Jason (a friend of mine) and I went to an Easter banquet. Yes, a banquet in prison. At least that was what they called it. To us, it was free food that wasn't prepared by the state. *It was street food.* There was chicken, potato salad, pie, etc. The Christian brothers put this event together as they celebrated the resurrection of Jesus Christ. At the time, all I could remember was the food was great.

The next year rolled around and it was time for the Easter banquet. Of course Jason and I wanted to attend. This year we had a friend, Tracey, who wanted to go with us. We asked Johnny (one of the inmates who kind of ran things over there in the chapel) if he would sign us up for the banquet again. It was limited seating, so you had to sign up. He checked with Henry (another inmate), who actually was in charge. Henry told Johnny that we had to attend one chapel service to sign up for the banquet. We didn't have to attend a service the year before; Johnny just signed us up.

That one service changed my life. Tracey's and Jason's lives were impacted as well. Henry was doing a life sentence for burglary under the California three-strikes-(your-out) law and was the one bringing the message that day.

The one thing I remember most about the message he gave was this: He held up his Bible in his hand and said, "I don't think this is the Word of God." *He paused*, and then he said, "I know this is the Word of God. Just because my finite little mind can't figure out an infinite God doesn't mean this isn't the Word of God." That one statement changed my whole outlook about the Word of God.

I used to pick and choose what I believed about the Bible. It wasn't until Henry spoke those words that I realized I didn't believe in God. *I doubted His Word.*

The thing about God's word is, it is all truth. You don't get to pick and choose what you think is true and what isn't. That is doubt! The Bible talks about doubt: "If any of you lacks wisdom, let him ask of God, who gives to all liberally and without reproach, and it will be given to him. But let him ask in faith, with no doubting, for he who doubts is like a wave of the sea driven and tossed by the wind. For let not that man suppose that he will receive anything from the Lord, he is a double-minded man, unstable in all his ways" (James 1:5–8).

So if you're going to doubt God's Word, don't expect Him to reveal anything to you. I realized I wasn't trusting what the Bible said. It was no wonder He didn't reveal His truth to me. I doubted it! Why should I expect anything from Him?

It was at that moment I asked God to forgive me and for Him to reveal His truth to me. He has been faithful to do so, and continues to. It's like a light switch has been turned on in my life, and His Word is illuminating me daily.

I found myself in my cell for hours on end reading God's Word. Since I didn't even like to read, that was a miracle in of itself. God is faithful! When I asked Him to forgive me and to give me wisdom, He held true to His promise. He opened up His Word to me and gave me understanding of it.

I don't claim to know it all *(you can believe that)*, but what I do know is, God has changed my life! It's only because I believe *all* of His Word now. Henry was right! Just because I can't figure out everything there is to know about the Bible doesn't mean it's not true.

I have lots of stories about my past, but in no way am I glorying in them. Actually, I am ashamed of them. "For when you were slaves of sin, you were free in regard to righteousness. What fruit did you have then in the things of which you are now ashamed; for the end of those things is death" (Romans 6:20–21).

In other words, when I didn't believe in God or His Word, I could care less about doing anything that was right. I did what I wanted, not caring whom I hurt or who got in my way. I'm ashamed of those things now, and I thank God for saving me from myself. God's Word and His spirit in me have truly set me free from the wicked things I once boasted about.

A person can choose to believe or reject God's Word. God is not going to force it on anyone. But it doesn't change the fact that it is true. I know it to be true! I can say that with conviction, because what I once did, I no longer do. I was a slave to sin, but not anymore. God has set me free!

I could not stop shooting drugs, stealing, etc. I truly was in bondage to sin, and Satan loved it. But I have good news, and it comes in the way of Jesus.

In the gospel of John, it says, "And a slave does not abide in the house forever, but a son abides forever. Therefore if the Son makes you free, you shall be free indeed" (John 8:35–36). Jesus set me free from sin and eternal death, and He wants to do the same for you.

I would encourage you to stop right now and pick up a Bible or go online. Find the gospel of John and read chapter 8, verses 31 through 47. There is life and death mentioned in those few verses. *I pray that you find and choose life.* I could quote those verses for you, but then I would be putting in the work. I already know the truth and have been set free. How badly do you want the truth? How badly do you want to be set free from sin? Is it something you want? Only you can answer that. The answers are in the Bible.

In the introduction of this book, I said this was a short story of my life. I lied! It is a short story of my life, but it really isn't my story. *It is God's story!* It's how He changed me from the inside out and has given me the desire to seek Him and what is good.

Everyone has desires. I did and still do. I have to ask myself every day, am I living a life pleasing to God, or am I living to please myself? When I lived to please myself, everyone around me knew it. That's because in one way or another, I hurt everyone close. I really didn't care either. That was the sad thing about it.

As a Christian, the last thing I want to do is sin against God. Some say a Christian shouldn't sin, and I would agree. No one should sin. But no one is without sin. Christians are not perfect; they are forgiven. "Therefore by the deeds of the law no flesh will be justified in His sight, for by the law is the knowledge of sin" (Romans 3:20).

God's commandments were given to show us that we are sinners and that we need a savior. They also reveal God's character, His holiness, and His standards. However, keeping the law perfectly will not make you right with God. Whether you're good or bad isn't the issue. *The forgiveness of sins through Jesus is.* The best you have to offer God is not good enough, and your worst isn't enough to keep you away from the love He has for you.

I'm sure you've noticed I quote the Bible a lot. In order to fall in love with someone, you have to get to know them. The way I fell in love with God was by reading His Word. If you get into His Word for yourself, you'll find yourself falling in love with Him as well.

I can remember when I used to see a pretty woman walk by and say, either to myself, or someone that was with me, "I love her." I had it all wrong; it wasn't love. I didn't even know her. It was lust. The difference between love and lust is that love gives and lust wants.

When you truly love someone, don't you want to serve them? You want to do things for them. You're willing to lavish them with gifts. When it comes to spending your time with them, there isn't enough time in a day.

Once you receive the love of God in your heart, you'll make sacrifices you never thought you would—all because of love! "God so *loved* the world that He *gave* His only begotten Son, that whoever believes in Him should not perish but have everlasting life" (John 3:16, emphasis added). That is one of many verses in the Bible that reveals what true love is. *God loved and gave! He gave His only Son to die for us.*

What do you love? Some people love things; they devote their time, money, energy, etc., into things. I'm not saying material things are bad. I'm saying to love them is. God wants our love. Once we give Him our love, then He will provide the things we need.

CHAPTER SEVEN

War Stories

SITTING AROUND IN PRISON TELLING war stories about how we used to rob, steal, and (for some) kill was our daily routine in prison. I was doing a little ninety-day parole violation at Chino State Prison for a dirty drug test. That was when I met this guy who was an engineer on the streets. He was a very smart guy and had never been in any kind of real trouble in his life.

He decided to drink and drive one day and killed someone in the process. He was convicted of vehicular manslaughter and was doing six years. He was Dead Eye's bunkie; Dead Eye was a friend of mine I had known for years. Dead Eye, whose real name was Steve, got that handle because he was missing one eye and it was replaced with a glass eye.

In prison, you meet a lot of different guys. I would say most are acquaintances and not real friends. Steve was a friend that had my back if need be. I remember one time when we were both out on the streets and I hadn't seen him for a while. He came by on Christmas and brought me a gift. Even though he was strung out, he still took the time to come by and say hi, bearing gifts. He probably stole the shirt he got me, but they say it is the thought that counts, right?

One day, Dead Eye and I were sitting around his bunk area along with his bunkie, the engineer. We were telling different stories of the crimes we had once done. This engineer said to me, "Larry, do you want to make a million bucks?"

I was thinking this was a pretty smart guy and he was going to give me game on how to make a million bucks. Of course I said, "Yes, I want to make a million bucks!" He replied, "Write a book." I thought this guy wasn't too smart after all. I don't even like to read. Even though I thought he was crazy, I had to hear more. I asked him, "Write a book about what?" His reply was, "The different stories of things you've done in your past."

This guy was fascinated at the stories we told. He couldn't believe some of the things we used to do to get what we wanted in life. *I mean some low-down stuff.* I can't believe some of the things we used to do. I haven't seen Steve in years and don't know what happened to him, but I can only imagine what he is up to: probably doing a life sentence.

Back in the early seventies, they used to have a telethon they ran annually. It was to raise money for the physically challenged. The only reason I tell this story is so you can see what God has delivered me from. *I am so ashamed of this.*

It was about 2:00 A.M. when I was watching this telethon on TV. I was sick as a dog! I hadn't shot up any heroin for hours and was suffering withdrawals. All of a sudden, I saw this one segment on how different people were raising money for this charity. People were going door-to-door, asking for donations. That was when I came up with a brainstorm. Have you noticed I have a lot of brainstorms; Stupid ones!

I figured I could raise money for my charity, *the "get-Larry-well" campaign.* I was too proud and ashamed to go door-to-door myself, so I enlisted my girlfriend to do it. She used to be a nurse's aide and still had her nurse's uniform in the closet. I told her to put her uniform on and to hit the streets. Of course she was hooked on heroin as well, which gave her the motivation to do it.

We went to a street that was close to the dope dealers house. Actually, it was the same street the connection lived on. While sitting there in his garage, along with some other dope fiend friends of mine, they saw my girlfriend going door-to-door, wondering what was up.

They started to ask me, "What is your girl friend doing?" I explained she was collecting money for my charity. They couldn't believe it! Everyone thought I was crazy. And to be honest, I would have to agree. But when she came back with seventy bucks from knocking on twenty doors or so, they were all thinking to themselves, *Why didn't we think of that?*

I bought some heroin, and we proceeded to get well. That was what we called it when we got our fix, *get well.* Once we both got well, I said to my girlfriend, "Get back out there." It was only a matter of minutes before the police were called and the cops jacked her up. Someone had become suspicious and called the authorities. The police didn't arrest her and really couldn't stop her from doing it either, but at that point, she had enough of that. I couldn't blame her.

That was my mentality; I didn't care who did what or who got cheated. I didn't even care if someone got hurt. I wanted my shot! Sure, if my girlfriend had gotten busted, I would have been bummed out, but at least I got well.

These were the kind of stories we would tell one another in prison. Then as we heard one another's stories, we would learn from one another's mistakes and glean from the successes. It's a sad thing to say, but I actually gloried in those things.

Believe me when I say, I'm not writing this book to try and make a million bucks. That is not my motive. Heck, I'll be lucky if one person reads it. But if that one person does read it and he or she gives their life to the Lord because of it, then my purpose has been accomplished. God has given me this task to share His goodness and His love with all those that are caught up in the kind of lifestyle I once lived. There is a way out, and *Jesus is that way!*

There was a big void in my life, and that void was not having God. I was empty inside. I thought putting drugs, alcohol, women, etc., into my life would make me happy. I sincerely believe it was the drugs, alcohol, etc. that brought me the unhappiness. God has replaced the drugs, alcohol, etc., with His love. That love has now manifested itself in the way I now live my life. It's not all about me, but about God and others. There is true fulfillment in my life, and I am so thankful to God for that.

God made us to be dependent creatures, but He wants us to depend on Him, not on drugs, alcohol, sex, or whatever else you're in bondage to. When your life feels empty, it's probably because it is. Don't try to fill it with the things that will lead to your destruction. Fill your life with God! "Do not be drunk with wine, in which is dissipation, but be filled with the spirit" (Ephesians 5:18). God wants to fill you with His Spirit, but you have to ask. He won't come into your life unless you invite Him in.

With over fifty arrests and close to that many convictions, I have a lot of war stories. That isn't counting the ones *I thought* I got away with. There are too many to tell, nor do I even care to tell. The ones I do share are a testimony as to what God has and is doing in my life. Not to mention His love and forgiveness toward me.

One of the craziest arrests I've encountered was just that, crazy! And it is one I'm grateful to still be alive.

CHAPTER EIGHT

Craziest of Crazy

IT WAS WHEN I WAS living in Oregon with my first wife and her two kids that I came across some money I had obtained illegally. We decided to make a road trip to Orange County, California. I wasn't using heroin when we lived in this small town for the simple fact there wasn't any there. I take that back. I wasn't strung out on heroin while living there. The truth is, from time to time I would make the hundred-mile journey to Klamath Falls to purchase heroin.

I realize as I look back on the events of this next story, even when I was in rebellion against God, He still watched over me and those around me.

As I said, we were on our way from Oregon to California for vacation. At least that was what we told the kids. Really it was to spend the thousand bucks I just stole on heroin. As we were making our way down south, I decided I needed to drink and drive, *another one of my smart moves.* We were driving a Chevy van when it happened, one of a parent's worst nightmares!

I'm traveling about ninety miles an hour on the I-5 Highway just outside of Bakersfield, California. All of a sudden, a car traveling in the slow lane decided to pass the semitruck he was behind. He was probably going fifty-five miles per hour when he pulled over into my lane. It was like pulling in front of a speeding bullet (me). There were only two lanes heading south in that section of the I-5. I swerved onto the middle shoulder of the road, having my two left wheels on gravel, and my right two still on the pavement passing the guy. In doing so, I never touched my brake pedal. As I passed him, I then turned my steering wheel to the right to get back onto the highway. My tires grabbed the road hard! It started pulling the van toward the right shoulder. I tried to pull out of it but was unable to. The van started rolling and rolling and rolling. I don't know how many times the van rolled; it seemed like an eternity. When it did stop, the van was on its wheels.

The two kids had been sleeping in the back when the incident happened. Once everything had settled, Cindy yelled out, "Where's Nicole?" The back doors to the van had flown open, and Nicole was missing. *We were terrified.*

I got out of the van and started to look for Nicole when I saw her walking up toward the van. She didn't know what happened. Thanks to God, not even a scratch was on her. Her shoulder was hurt a little bit, but nothing was broken. That was what I meant when I said God still watched over me and those around me.

When the cops arrived, I was arrested for drunk driving and taken to jail. But that isn't the arrest I am talking about. That was just one that led up to the crazy one.

My parents drove from Orange County to Bakersfield to pick up Cindy and the kids from the hospital. I was released from jail eight hours later, and we all went to my mom and dad's house. We ended up staying there for a couple of weeks until I ran out of the money I originally started with and was out of options. I think my mom was tired of us all at this point. She decided to loan me the money to buy a cheap car to get us back to Oregon.

Looking back and reflecting on these stories, I realize just how irresponsible I really was. Drugs take you so far out of reality and in your own little world of self. *You think of nobody but yourself.* The Bible teaches about putting others first and to actually deny yourself. At that stage of my life, I thought only of myself.

During those two weeks in Orange County, I was using heroin every day. Now strung out on heroin and having only a couple of grams of heroin left, we decided to head back to Oregon. We arrived in Oregon, and it was home sweet home—*that is, until I ran out of heroin.* I was sick and wanted to get well.

After a couple of days into the withdrawals, I decided I was going back to Orange County to get well. Why drive 750 miles to get well? I don't know, but that was what I started out to do. I was driving down the I-5, going about eighty-five miles an hour. *Obviously, I didn't learn much from my previous speeding incident a couple of weeks earlier.* Out of the blue, a highway patrolman was behind me and red-lights me. I had a bottle of booze which I shoved under the front seat. I also had a syringe in my front pocket that I didn't know what to do with.

When I pulled over, it was on an off-ramp just outside of a little town called Willows, California. The officer approached my car and instructed me to step out of the vehicle. He could smell alcohol on me and wanted to search the car. When I opened the door to get out, he could visually see the bottle of booze sticking out from under the front seat. Good stash job! As he went down to reach for the bottle of booze, I reached into my front pocket and pulled the syringe out and threw it over the top of the car down into the shrubs on the side of the road. *Got away with another one.* When I say that, I'm being facetious. I didn't get away with anything. God sees everything we do. The Bible talks about how our sins are recorded in a book in heaven. *Something for us to think about.*

At this point, the officer walked me back to the hood of his car. He proceeded to pat me down to check for weapons or anything illegal. Too late for that; I already got rid of the syringe. He then radioed in my driver's license information to run a warrant check.

As the officer was writing me a ticket for speeding, he was waiting to hear from dispatch with wants and warrants. I was standing right beside the officer as he was writing the ticket when it came over the radio: "Code 1036M." I had no idea what that meant at the time. I did know I had warrants out of Kern County for the drunk driving and for a petty theft warrant out of Orange County.

The 1036M code stands for confidential information, possible misdemeanor wants. In other words, this guy was wanted, and one should stand clear of him and be on alert. The officer responded back to dispatch, "Code 4," letting dispatch know it was OK to relay the information. *It wasn't!* Dispatch started to inform the officer of the wants out of both counties. That was when I grabbed the officer's gun. What was I thinking? I wasn't! I just knew I was sick and that jail would prevent me from getting well.

Prior to the radio transmission about the wants for me, there was radio contact from another officer to the officer that was with me. He relayed to him that he was on his way to our location for backup. I knew help was coming, and I had to make a quick decision as to what I was going to do.

Obviously, I made a very bad one and regret it to this day. I do not recommend this to anyone. It has haunted me ever since.

The officer and I were struggling for control of the weapon when I realized he was not going to let go. There were a hundred things going through my mind at this point in time. I knew I had to hurry because this other officer was going to be showing up any minute. I was much bigger than the officer I was struggling with and had an advantage over him in that regard, but he had a death grip on this gun. I didn't want to shoot this cop. I just wanted to get well.

I had control of the handle and trigger and could very well have put a bullet in his belly. As we were still struggling for the gun, I realized I couldn't get it out of his hands. I figured that if I fired one shot, maybe the muzzle flash and the heat would cause him to let go. This struggle was going back and forth. He was pulling; I was pulling. At times, the barrel of the gun was pointed at me, then it was pointed at him. Back and forth it went. I was not trying to get shot, and I was not trying to shoot anyone.

I saw what I thought was an opening to fire the gun without anyone getting shot. *Boom!* One shot was fired, and he let go. I moved away from him as quickly as possible. That was when I saw it in his eyes that he was going to try to come and get his gun back. I pointed the gun at him and yelled, "Freeze!" *Oh, how I thank God he froze and didn't come at me.* Who knows what would have happened. I'm pretty sure it wouldn't have been a good decision either.

I started to run to my car for a quick getaway when I realized he had a car too. Duh! *Boom, boom!* I fired two shots into the radiator of his car, thinking that would disable it; wrong again. Yes, it did put a couple of holes in the radiator, but he was still able to drive it.

I jumped into my car and took off. I thought I was getting back onto the highway, but it wasn't the on-ramp. It was an access road running parallel to the highway. It was a dirt road with dust flying up everywhere behind me like a dust storm. You couldn't see anything. I didn't know if he was behind me or not. I just knew I had to get away. I was probably going eighty or ninety miles an hour when the dirt road I was on made a sudden right turn. My car flew off into a ravine and crashed. It was out of commission, and I was stuck on this embankment.

I jumped out of the car and put the gun into my waistband. I started climbing up the embankment to get back up to the highway. Once I was on top, I started to run out onto Interstate I-5. I needed a car and wanted someone to give me theirs.

Cars were already slowing down prior to me running onto the freeway. Just about a month prior to this incident, there was approximately a hundred-car pileup on the I-5 due to a dust storm and lack of visibility. When people saw the dust from my car, they thought it was another dust storm.

One lady was stopped when she saw me coming toward her car. She must have seen the look of desperation on my face because she started rolling up the windows on her car and locking the doors.

I heard a loud bang and looked over to see the highway patrol officer there with a shotgun in his hands. This was the same officer I just had the encounter with. He chased me down in the same car I just shot up.

I ran across the middle median of the road that had a bunch of oleander bushes. I ran through them, and now I had a blocked view from the officer. I then ran to the other side of oncoming traffic, which was also slowed by this time. I removed the gun from my waistband and threw it as hard as I could into a big field where there was a bunch of weeds and bushes.

Mind you, I was really thinking on my feet by this time (yeah right). The reason for throwing the gun was in hopes they wouldn't find it. *If they don't find the gun,* I was thinking, *how can anyone say I took something they can't find?* Real logic, huh? They did find the gun with my fingerprints on it.

Now on the opposite side of the highway, a truck ended up stopping. I ran over to him and opened his door. I tried to pull him out of his truck, but this guy was huge; it wasn't happening. I gave up on that idea pretty quick.

At this point, I think I realized the jig was up. The highway patrolman was now maybe twenty yards from me with his shotgun, ordering me to the ground. I looked over to the one lady that had rolled up her windows. She was still sitting there on the highway. That was when I saw her kind of pleading with me to get down on the ground.

I gave up and was taken to jail and charged. They booked me into jail for attempted murder, removing a firearm from a peace officer, brandishing a weapon, attempted robbery for trying to pull that guy out of his truck, shooting an unoccupied vehicle, and drunk driving. Needless to say, I went to prison for that little escapade and was transported to San Quentin State Prison after sentencing.

That is just one reason why I am so thankful to still be alive. God has been so gracious and merciful to me. I sure wasn't deserving of His grace and mercy. The only thing any of us deserve is death. We have all sinned, and the penalty is death. It is only because of God's grace and mercy that we can have life in Jesus Christ.

Maybe you have never done anything of this magnitude and feel I should have been killed that day. I would have to say you're probably right. That's why I thank God every time I think about it. *God spared my life that day.* God's mercy and love endure forever!

Read the Bible and check out some of the stories in it about different people who made some pretty bad decisions too. God not only spared them but also used them to write about it in His Word. God uses foolish things and foolish people for His purpose and His glory. And he wants to use you too!

CHAPTER NINE

Ashamed

WHEN JESUS CAME INTO MY life about twelve years ago, I was doing a thirteen-year prison sentence. It was a moment in my life that I will never forget. I knew I was a different person! But still I was ashamed, and it wasn't of my sin; it was of Christ.

I knew God wanted me to go to church. But I was in prison, and I didn't want the other inmates to think I was some kind of weak Bible-thumping Christian. I didn't want people to see me carrying a Bible across the prison yard to go to church. There was no other explanation except that I was ashamed of Christ. Peer pressure is real, and I can relate to what our young kids have to deal with on a daily basis.

Fear can motivate us to make wrong decisions. If we *will* fear God rather than man, then the choices we make in life will be better ones. "And do not fear those who kill the body but cannot kill the soul. But rather fear Him who is able to destroy both soul and body in hell" (Matthew 10:28). I feared man rather than God, and it showed in my actions.

One day, as I was walking across the yard to go to church, my brother in Christ (Henry) set me up. I'm sure he didn't see it that way, and I never told him, but looking back on it now, I see it as a Holy Spirit setup. As we were walking over to the church, he was carrying his Bible. He had some papers and other stuff he was fumbling around with as well. He reached out and handed me his Bible. He asked me to carry it for him. *I almost froze in my tracks!* I was thinking at this point, *It's bad enough that I'm walking across the yard with a Christian, and now you want me to carry a Bible too!* I took it and carried it across the yard for everyone to see. *Wow, what a milestone.* It was a terrifying experience, to be honest.

My entire life revolved around me wanting to be a gangster. To be a gangster, you have to walk the walk and talk the talk. I thank God for that moment in time when Henry handed me his Bible. It really was a milestone in my new walk with the Lord.

Later in my Christian walk, I found a verse in the Bible that became one of my many favorites and memory verses: "For I am not ashamed of the gospel of Christ, for it is the power of God to salvation for everyone who believes, for the Jew first and also for the Greek" (Romans 1:16). God is the one who saved me from death and delivered me from the power of sin. It wasn't those guys walking the prison yard. I was no longer ashamed of my God and Savior Jesus Christ.

It wasn't too long after that when I was tested in that area of my life. I was at the drinking fountain over by the weight pile when I was talking to two of my old buddies. When I say *old*, I don't mean in age, but old friends that I really didn't have much in common with anymore now that I was a Christian. I can't remember what the conversation was about, but one of my new Christian friends came walking up and joined in the conversation.

I had said something that was obviously a blessing from God, and Johnny (the Christian friend) replied, "Thank God for that!" One of my old friends said, "Yeah, Larry, thank God for that." It wasn't what he said; it was the way he said it—with sarcasm! At first I was embarrassed, but just for a split second. Then I said with a stern voice, "Yeah, I do thank God for that!" It wasn't what I said, but how I said it that got my old friend's attention. It was with a hint of, *"What are you going to do about it?"* in my voice. They were kind of surprised at my response but actually respected it and didn't say anything else about it.

One thing about doing time in prison is, if you show weakness, they will prey on you like a pit bull on a pork chop. When I was living for the devil I wasn't afraid of anyone, so why should I be now? The only thing that has changed is I'm serving the living God instead of the defeated devil. God tested my faith that day, and (it is) thanks to Him I had the courage to speak up and give Him thanks.

A little thing like speaking out and saying thanks to God in that situation really made a difference in my life. Hopefully, it made an impact on the two old friends of mine as well. Having the boldness to make such a simple statement will hopefully empower them to one day stand up and say; *thank God* to someone they know.

My faith has been tested in other areas of my life as well, and to be quite honest, I have failed more than once. That can be discouraging to say the least, but there is an assurance of God finishing the work He has begun. "Being confident of this very thing, that He who has begun a good work in you will complete it until the day of Jesus Christ" (Philippians 1:6). So until Jesus returns to this earth as He has promised, God is doing a good work in our life. He isn't going to stop in the middle. He will complete what He starts—unlike me! It seems as though I can't ever finish anything I start.

We all sin and fall short of God's perfection. Our focus and attention should be on the good things God is doing in our life and not on the bad things we once did. Satan wants to keep us in bondage to our old thoughts and failures. God wants to renew our minds, and He does that through His Word.

I can remember one time while in my bedroom; I was all strung out on heroin hating life. I wanted to be free from drugs, but had no clue on how to get off of them. I had a bible in my dresser drawer, and I knew deep down in my heart that God could help me. Every once in a while, I would pull the Bible out of the drawer and hold it close to me. I would ask God to help me. That was a good start, asking God to help me. Too bad that was where it ended. I never opened the Bible to read God's Word. God will and does help us when we ask. Usually that help comes through the reading of His Word. Your

Bible will do you no good sitting in a dresser drawer or sitting on a shelf. And when you do read it, it's important to believe it as well. That's when the help will come.

Believing in God's Word will work in us effectively. "For this reason we also thank God without ceasing, because when you received the word of God which you heard from us, you welcomed it not as the word of men, but as it is in truth, the word of God, *which also effectively works in you who believe*" (1 Thessalonians 2:11, emphasis added). If we don't believe in what God says, then don't expect God to do anything.

Everyone has faith or believes in something. Just because someone believes in something doesn't mean it is true. For instance, I can believe a certain football team will win the game, but it doesn't mean it will. It may, but there is no guarantee. If you believe in God's Word, you can trust it to be true, and God will do what He says! God does change the hearts of men and women, and He wants to change yours.

Actually, the Bible teaches that the Word of God will change your heart. It will soften some, and for others, it will harden. I found this one verse in the Bible that says, "Now by this we know that we know Him [God] if we keep His commandments" (1 John 2:3). The word *commandment* has a really profound meaning. It means authoritative prescription. Keep in mind that the New Testament was originally written in Greek, so you have to go to a Greek/English dictionary to get the proper meaning.

Authoritative prescription! When I think of a prescription, having a drug history, I think of nothing else but drugs. When a doctor orders a prescription for a patient with an infection, it is usually an antibiotic. Now that person's body will either respond to, or react to that drug. When the body responds, it gets better. When it reacts, it gets worse.

I'm allergic to two different kinds of antibiotics. When I take them, my body has a reaction to them. I break out in a rash, and the infection just gets worse. When given a different type of antibiotic, my body responds to it, and I get better. *It's the same with the Word of God.* You either respond to God's authoritative prescription or you react to it.

To respond to God's Word would be to read it, believe it, trust it, and live it. To react would be to read it, not believe it, not trust it, not live it. So my question to you would be; are you responding to, or reacting to God's authoritative prescription? Do you want to get better? Or are you cool with your disease? You know, the one the Bible calls sin? Sin (which leads to death) or Jesus (who gives life)? It's really your choice!

CHAPTER TEN

Believing

IN THE PREVIOUS CHAPTER, I said that to respond to God's Word would be to read it, believe it, trust it, and live it. *The truth is, I don't always live it.* I believe in God and His Word with all my heart. I want to live it every moment of my life, but the fact remains that I don't all the time.

Every Christian is in a battle. That battle is a spiritual one. Satan is as real as God is, and he does not want you to serve God. The truth is, Satan wants to be god and he wants you to serve him. I touched on that earlier in the book, quoting, "Who are you a slave to: either sin leading to death or righteousness leading to God?"

Even when we understand we're in a spiritual battle, we tend to forget we are. That's because we can't see the spirits that are kind of behind the scenes, if you will. Because we can't see them, a lot of people won't even acknowledge they exist. *That is just another ploy of Satan.* If he can get you to doubt God's Word, then he's won the battle already.

There is a story in the Bible where one angel killed 185,000 people in one night. Don't think angels aren't powerful; they are! That's why we need God on our side when these spiritual attacks come.

If you're a child of God, a born-again believer, guess what that makes you? An enemy of Satan! You are now enlisted in the army of God and are in the battle. That is why the Bible tells us to "put on the whole armor of God that you may be able to stand against the wiles of the devil, for we do not wrestle against flesh and blood, but against principalities, against powers, against the rulers of the darkness of this age, against spiritual hosts of wickedness in the heavenly places" (Ephesians 6:11–12). In plain words, the *heavenly places* means "all around us."

I used to say that if I could see Satan, I think I could take him. Without God, I don't stand a chance, and that has been proven. Satan has whooped me up more times than I can count. This is why we need to keep the armor of God on at all times. *The devil wants to destroy us.* "Be sober, be vigilant, because your adversary the devil walks about like a roaring lion, seeking whom he may devour" (1 Peter 5:8).

This is real stuff, and you need to know it. When we keep God's armor on, that is when we have God's protection. It doesn't mean we won't be taking hits from the enemy; we will. I took a hit, and it was a hard one, one of the hardest I've taken since being a Christian. It came in the form of marriage.

There are several pieces to the armor of God. One of those is the helmet of salvation. What does the helmet protect? The head! Surely someone can take a hit to the head and be fine. But if the mind is penetrated, then we have a problem. The biggest part of our battle is in the mind. If Satan can tempt us in a way that will cause us to act contrary to God's Word, or get us to believe his lies, then there will be damage.

I encourage you to check out what the whole armor of God is. Once you do, put it on and wear it even in your sleep. When soldiers are in a war out in the trenches, they don't take off their gear when they sleep. That's the attitude we're to have: *to be suited up at all times.* This armor I'm speaking about is in the book of Ephesians, chapter 6, verses 10 through 18.

With that being said, I took a hit to the mind. I determined in my mind that I wanted to find a wife. Not that it is a bad thing to find a wife. The Bible says, "He who finds a wife finds a good thing and obtains favor from the Lord" (Proverbs 18:22). But one has to ask oneself, why is it I want to get married, and is it for the right reason? Selfish motives are not the right reason for marriage.

I feel it necessary to expound a little more on the battle we're in. That battle has a lot to do with what lies within us. Jesus gives us a perfect example: "For from within, out of the [*heart*], that is [*mind, character, inner self, will, intentions, center*], proceed evil thoughts, adulteries, fornication, murders, thefts, covetousness, wickedness, deceit, lewdness, and evil eye, blasphemy, pride, foolishness. All these things come from within and defile a man" (Mark 7:21–23, emphasis added).

So from our heart-or our mind, for a better term, comes all these things. What we put into our mind is what is going to come out. If you put lustful thoughts in, lustful actions will manifest themselves in one way or another. That's why the Bible also tells us to renew our mind with the Word of God. If you put the Word of God in, good things will start to show in the way you live your life.

One more aspect of the Christian battle is the flesh against the Spirit. "Walk in the Spirit, and you shall not fulfill the lust of the flesh. For the flesh lusts against the Spirit and the Spirit against the flesh, and these are contrary to one another, so that you do not do the things that you wish. But if you are led by the Spirit, you are not under the law" (Galatians 5:16–18).

Remember that sin nature we inherited from Adam? That nature still lies within us and is battling with the Spirit of God that dwells in all Christians. That battle goes on day in and day out. We need to remind ourselves of that so we don't fall victim to our sinful thoughts.

My reason for marriage was to be intimate with a woman. My flesh wanted sex, and that was all there was to it. *Out of my heart flowed evil thoughts*. Fornication is evil, and that was exactly what I ended up doing.

I look back on it now and realize I didn't have the helmet of salvation on, which would have protected my mind. We have to protect our mind from our own imagination. When those thoughts come to mind, we need to cast them down to the obedience of Christ. Instead of protecting my mind with the helmet of salvation, I let my mind imagine what it would be like to be intimate with a woman. In doing so, I wasn't obedient to God's Spirit.

When I met my soon-to-be wife, I felt that I loved her, but I have to ask myself: Was it love or lust? I mentioned earlier in this book about lust, love, and the effects of both. I knew I was heading for a wreck because of the desires of my flesh, but I allowed those thoughts in. Marriage is good, and so is sex, but if you're seeking marriage just to have sex, I would have to testify that it is not for the right reason.

Instead of taking the whole counsel of God into account, I took one verse out of the Bible and made it fit into my *plans*. The entire Bible is the whole counsel of God, not just one verse. You can't build a doctrine or teaching on one verse. There are sixty-six books in the Bible, and to take one verse out of the entire Bible to make it fit into your scheme of things is wrong.

The bible gives specific instructions in regards to marriage; and even in whom to marry. When you marry outside of God's will, it's like trying to mix water and oil together. They don't mix! It became evident to me rather quickly that this marriage wasn't a match made in heaven. Looking back on it now, I think it was because we were both at different levels of faith in our walk with the Lord at that time. Maybe I expected too much. In my own mind; I felt she wasn't living the way a Christian woman should, and therefore I felt she wasn't a Christian at all. She wasn't the perfect woman I had anticipated, or expected.

A Christian friend once said to me: "I'm not the object of your faith, Jesus Christ is. If you hang around me long enough you're going to see something you don't like, or something you think isn't very Christian like. He went on to say: Jesus is the only One who is perfect, so you need to keep your eyes on Him. Not on me or others."

I thank God he told me that too. It wasn't but a couple of weeks later that what he said came to fruition. To this day I can't remember what it was that he did, but at the time I was ready to walk away from him and the church because of it. Then I remembered his words: "Jesus is the object of your faith, not me or others." People aren't perfect, even when we want them to be.

Here is a scripture that talks about ceasing from sin: "That he no longer should live the rest of his time in the flesh for the lusts of men, but for the will of God. For we have spent enough of our past lifetime in doing the will of the *Gentiles [or unbelievers]* when we walked in lewdness, lusts, drunkenness, revelries, drinking parties, and abominable idolatries" (1 Peter 4:2–3, emphasis added).

Do you see that *"spent enough of our past lifetime in doing bad"* is what it is basically saying? So what time we have here left on earth, we should live for God and not for ourselves or for the devil. It will only lead to destruction, and it's a lesson I'm still learning.

I guess when I've read that verse in the past, I only paid attention to the words *drunkenness, drinking parties, abominable idolatries.* I actually no longer participate in those. *I missed or chose to ignore the one on lust.* Lust got me into trouble, big trouble! If I had paid more attention to the Word of God instead of my own desires, I wouldn't have sought a wife for my own desires.

The relationship between my wife and I was in no way glorifying God. Now I felt I needed to get out of it before I fell back into my old way of living. I'm not saying it was right, but it is what I did.

At one point in our marriage, I found myself on the front porch with a can of beer in my hand. I was ready to pop the top and start drinking again. Drinking was one of the substances God delivered me from, and I was about to return to it. I was a total idiot when drunk. I thank God He stopped me in my tracks. God spoke to me in my *heart* at that very moment in time on the porch. He said, "What are you doing?" I took that can of beer and threw it to the ground, never to pick another one up. Don't get me wrong, not drinking, not smoking, not cursing, etc., doesn't make you a Christian. If that is the case, then I have a friend that has about ten dogs that are Christians. Those dogs don't drink, curse, smoke, etc. Get my point?

To be a Christian is to place your trust in Christ alone for your salvation. Salvation isn't based on what you think you can do to deserve it or earn it. God loves us the way we are, but He loves us too much to leave us that way. His Word and His Spirit in us will clean us up—that is, if we ask Him and allow Him to.

Our marriage wasn't the way God intended it. I don't know why I expected it to work. God has set boundaries in His Word, and I stepped over those boundaries when it came to me finding a wife for myself. Chalk up another failure in my life. In spite of all that, God worked it out for good. I will do a whole chapter on the subject of God working things out for good.

Remember, *I said the battle is in the mind.* So in my mind, I wanted to justify my actions of getting married. I told myself, "You were in prison for ten years and twenty-two days. You've been out of prison for two years now, and you know you want to be intimate with a woman. So when are you going to find a wife?"

I had this conversation with myself to get to the results I wanted. People do that, have conversations with themselves. It's only when you answer yourself that you have a problem. We need to be careful with our thoughts. They tend to get us into wrecks at times. Who am I kidding, speaking for myself, a lot of the time.

When a child is a minor and under the authority of his parents, he has to have permission to do certain things, right? Well, it is kind of the same way with the children of God. They need to ask God if certain things are okay.

I didn't wait for God to find me a wife; I found my own. It was in my own way and on my own terms. There are guidelines for finding a wife, and there are consequences when you don't follow them.

It was twelve years or so of being without the companionship of a woman. Actually, it was longer than that. Prior to my incarceration, I wasn't intimate with any woman for at least two years. Only because I was married to my heroin and cocaine addiction during that period. So fourteen years had passed since I had been with a woman.

I know it was wrong, but at the time it seemed right to get married so that we could get out of the sin of fornication. Don't ask me why I didn't just get out of the sin of fornication, but I didn't. After all, I did want to be married and figured this would solve our sin issue. Then we could have our cake and eat it too. Wrong! The bad thing is; not doing it God's way was *bad* for the both of us. It's amazing the things we can conjure up in our minds to get the results we hope for and want.

I knew what the scriptures said about marriage. I didn't apply them to my life, and it ended up in disaster. The reality of it is that I knew it was going to be all bad. I went and pursued the relationship anyway. Some might say that is crazy, and I would have to agree. You have to realize that is what the flesh wants to do when you don't put God into the equation. It goes back to that sin nature we inherited from Adam and Eve.

I know I can rest on the promises of God. And it's only His promises that give me the hope I do have. And that hope is that He will work all things out for good.

CHAPTER ELEVEN

All Things for Good

"AND WE KNOW THAT ALL things work together for good to those who love God, to those who are the called according to His purpose" (Romans 8:28). I love that verse! I guess it's because even in all my failures, mistakes, trials, and sins, God works these things out for good to those who love Him. Do you love God? If so, it is His promise to work all things out for good for you.

A guy in prison gave me this analogy, and it goes well with this verse. When you make chocolate chip cookies, it takes different ingredients to make them. You're going to need flour, salt, sugar, chocolate chips, eggs, etc.

After you mix all these ingredients together, put them on a cookie sheet, and bake them at 350 degrees for eight to ten minutes, you come out with the best-tasting cookies ever.

Suppose you were to eat one ingredient at a time. Do you think the flour would taste good by itself? What about the salt? Maybe you would like the raw eggs by themselves? Some would agree that the chocolate chips might taste good by themselves. Others might say raw sugar would taste good. I guess that would be up to each individual on what would taste good or bad.

That's kind of what God does with the believer's life. He allows good and bad things to happen. It's a reality! *Good and bad things happen.* But His promise is to turn them all into good. The Bible verse says "all things," not just some. God has proven His Word to be true on more than one occasion in my life.

God is omniscient, meaning He knows all things. I made a big mess of things when I got into a relationship for the purpose of my own lustful desires. Did God know I was heading for a wreck? You better believe it! God allowed it not because He approved of it, but because He has given us free will. He gives us the freedom of choice. Sometimes we choose wrong things. When I chose to go outside of God's will, the world as I knew it started to fall apart.

When Jesus was about to go to the cross to die for our sins, He prayed to the Father in heaven and said, "O My father, if it is possible, let this cup pass from Me, nevertheless, not as I will, but as You will" (Matthew 26:39b). Jesus was the perfect example of perfect obedience. The love Jesus has for us and for the Father led Him to the cross. He gave His life so that we might have life. Our love for God will lead us to obedience as well. Obedience should be done out of love, not out of compulsion. When you do things out of love, that thing you're doing isn't so hard to do.

We love so many things in life. We love money, success, or fame. Whatever it is, we love it. Our love should be directed toward God and not things. When we love Him and seek Him, He will bless us in return. That's just who God is. But God will also take away. He took away what I really loved most in my life, and that was the teaching of His Word. My love was misdirected, and God gave me what I thought I wanted. When He did, *I was the most miserable person ever.*

When a person is born again; he or she has the Spirit of God in them. When he or she falls into sin, God's Spirit in them will convict them of their sin. A better term for the word convict, would be, convince.

It kind of works like this: God's Spirit in that person convinces them what they are doing is wrong and gives the person a choice. At the time, I was teaching a men's bible study on Sunday mornings. *I know, huh!* It saddens my heart thinking about my foolishness. So

God's Spirit in me was convicting me-saying: Do you want to continue practicing sin, or do want to continue teaching my word? God gave me the choice!

I chose to stop the teaching. At that point in my life, I guess I loved my sin more than God. I can't give any other explanation other than that. Once I quit teaching, other good things started to disappear as well.

Months earlier, I had applied to be approved to go into juvenile hall for the purpose of ministering to troubled kids. God took that away by having the probation department deny me approval for that ministry. I really see that as God saying to me, You want to live in sin, then don't expect to do the things I've called you to do. Also I was entrusted with the keys and alarm codes to all our church buildings, which I relinquished; due to fact I quit teaching. It brings me to tears writing about it.

Slowly I was giving up everything I loved, all for the sake of what I will call a fling. But God is true and faithful to His Word. *He never left me or forsook me.* He took the mess I made and turned it into good.

Prior to getting married and still to this day, I have been blessed with my own business. Thank God He didn't take that too. Really I was deserving of that loss as well. I say that because I was procrastinating in paying my taxes. I was never in the position where I had to file my own taxes or had the knowledge on how to do it. I had intentions of filing them, but I was using the "I don't know how to" excuse to put it off.

I'm talking about myself here, and I want to keep it real. You can make all the excuses you want to. We can justify things in our own mind to do or not to do something. But for me, I knew it was sin, and I was allowing it in my life. And yes, the Spirit of God in me was convincing me that it was sin, yet I chose not to listen! There is no excuse for sin to be in any believer's life, especially as a Bible teacher!

I had been deceived and wasn't obedient to God. "But be doers of the word, and not hearers only, deceiving yourselves" (James 1:22).

I was hearing God's Word but not applying it to all areas of my life. And to be honest, I still fall short of God's glory.

Going to church and hearing God's Word will not save you. Maybe the following verse will help you understand what it means to be saved. "Therefore lay aside all filthiness and overflow of wickedness, and *receive* with meekness the implanted word, which is able to save your souls" (James 1:21, emphasis added). The Bible is the written Word of God. As children of God, we need to live it out in our lives. Good works can't save us, but God did create us for them.

I look back on it now and see that God was working things out for good even when I was in a bad marriage. God used my wife to *convince* me to start paying my taxes. God uses different people to do different things for His purpose. I thank God He used her to lead me in the right direction.

I was still continuing to make one bad decision after another—correction, one sin after another! I think it was Adrian Rogers who said, "Sin will take you down the road further than you want to go, keep you longer than you want to stay, and cost you more than you want to spend."

Instead of focusing my love toward God, I was focusing my lust for my wife. *It just wasn't working out for good.* The more I wanted from her, the less I got. When I chose to get into this relationship, I knew it wasn't God's will. God's will is far better than any of our wants.

I heard a recorded message from Adrian Rogers yesterday. He said, "The most miserable person in the world isn't an unbeliever. It is a believer out of fellowship with God." That is so true! Once you know Jesus Christ as your Lord and Savior and fall into sin, it makes you miserable. Don't you wish sin would make all people miserable? We sure would have a lot less crime in the world today.

People have the attitude, "*So-and-so does it*, so why can't I?" I'm guilty of that as well. That is a lie straight from the pit of hell! Sin is wrong, and it always will be. There is good news though. It is as simple as confessing it, repenting of it, and allowing God to start working things out for good in your life again.

When a person bumps his head on something, it usually hurts. He doesn't purposely continue to do it. We need to remove the things we are bumping our heads on in life. Sin hurts, and it causes us pain! However, once the sin is removed, we then need to replace it with God's Word.

Being in this marriage was like me bumping my head over and over again. The pain we cause ourselves sometimes is just crazy. My hopes were by getting married it would draw her closer to God. Six months into the marriage, we decided to file for divorce.

As for me, I felt that my relationship with God was more important than any bad marriage. To some, that may not make sense, but once a person has tasted and seen God's goodness, it is a terrible thing to be out of fellowship with God. The morning my wife and I went down to the courthouse together to file for divorce was a sad day for the both of us. Looking back at it now, I think we gave up on each other to quickly. I think our focus was on each other, instead of Jesus. The one thing we both did agree on; was the fact that God would forgive us. It doesn't justify our actions, but it does bring comfort to know God still loves us in spite of our failure.

After filing for divorce, I was too ashamed to go back to my old church. I started attending another one and talked to the pastor within the first week. I told him about my situation, and he encouraged me and welcomed me into their church. God welcomes sinners into His church; it is full of them. So don't let that hinder you from walking into one.

Don't get me wrong; it wasn't that I wasn't welcome at my previous church: I was. Both Pastors came to my house on more than one occasion to convey that to me. The love and concern they had for me and my well being is an awesome testimony of God's people. As much as I wanted to go back, I was just too ashamed. To face all the people who attended my wedding was too much for me to bear. It was a terrible feeling.

I am no longer teaching a Bible study but am now sitting in the pews, being taught all over again. At least that is the way I felt. I was definitely humbled by the mess I had created for myself. I knew I needed to turn back to God and seek His guidance. We make mistakes, but God doesn't! God made us, and when He did, He said it was good. "Then God saw everything that He had made, and indeed it was very good. So the evening and the morning were the sixth day" (Genesis 1:31). God doesn't make junk, so don't ever let Satan tell you that you are. When I say Satan, I mean other people he will sometimes use to speak for him, if you know what I mean. My dad used to tell me I was worthless.

As I was being humbled and seeking God again instead of my own desires, God kept another one of His promises. "Therefore humble yourselves under the mighty hand of God, that He may exalt you in due time, casting all your care upon Him, for He cares for you" (1 Peter 5:6–7).

God did stop using me for a season. But God is faithful to His Word and says that if you humble yourselves, He will lift you up. And lift me up He did! God is so good and so faithful. It blows my mind how good and faithful He really is.

God took my shame, my brokenness, and my failure, and mixed it with His love. And when He did, out came the best tasting *cookies* ever.

CHAPTER TWELVE

Restoration

FOUR YEARS HAVE PASSED, AND I love the new church I now attend. I've also been attending an evangelism ministry at Calvary Chapel Chino Hills. The name of that ministry is *The Call*. This ministry is based on the teaching from the book, 'Evangelism Explosion' by D. James Kennedy.

I've come to meet and know many God-fearing Christians in this evangelism ministry. They have taught me how to share God's good news with people I've never met. The good news is that eternal life is free! God wants to give it to every human being created. I knew this but had never been trained on how to share it with total strangers.

God is working things out for good in my life. God is using me to lead people to Jesus Christ for the salvation of their souls. As a Bible teacher, I never led anyone to Jesus. People are coming to know how to receive the gift of eternal life through this ministry. I don't understand why God would use a dirt clod like me to share His gift with others, but I thank Him that He does. God is so faithful!

The pastor at my new church, Pastor Paul, was interested in bringing this evangelism ministry from Chino Hills down to Orange County. We started The Way ministry at Calvary Chapel Life on January 25, 2016. It is the same ministry as *The Call*; we just changed the name. God is restoring what I had forfeited. He is giving me another chance. Failure is not final when you're a child of God.

Some might argue, what is so good about serving God and going out to tell others about God? Let me pose this question to you: Which would be better, my going out to tell people how God loves them and how He offers them His free gift of eternal life, or me putting a gun in people's faces telling them to give me everything they have? You make the call: which is right, and which is wrong?

God has not forsaken me as His Word promises. He continues to work in my life. I'm caught up on paying my income taxes with my metal business, *past and present*. I actually know how to prepare the taxes myself now. Now that my taxes are being reported, it shows I have an income, which has led me to establishing excellent credit. I didn't have any credit prior to my relationship with my wife. My business has since increased and is blessed even more so today.

I don't want to be misunderstood; my happiness isn't based on what I have or don't have. My joy only comes from Christ and His faithfulness. Jesus is teaching me to love as He loved the Father. That love is leading me to be obedient to Him. Jesus said, "If you love Me, keep My commandments" (John 14:15).

I no longer have a wife, *but my fellowship with God is restored*. He will always be first in my life, and I wouldn't want it any other way. I learned that my way isn't the best God has for me. Who knows, God willing, *He* will bring me a wife that loves Him more than she could ever love me. If a wife loves God more than her husband, then the husband will have nothing to worry about. Her love for God will be revealed in her love for her husband as well. Guaranteed!

Things aren't perfect in my life by any means, but God is continuing to work these things out for good. I do know that I don't ever want to bump my head like that again.

CHAPTER THIRTEEN

Dead Man Walking

KIND OF AN OXYMORONIC TITLE for a chapter in a book, wouldn't you agree? After all, dead men can't walk, or can they? I'm here to tell you they can and I have seen it with my own eyes.

I was at San Quentin State Prison after my arrest and conviction for removing a firearm from a police officer and other various charges related to that incident. It was there where I saw the first dead man walking. It was quite a surreal feeling when I heard the guard shouting, "Dead man walking!" It was definitely an attention getter, to say the least. I thought to myself, *What the heck!*

When a person is sentenced to death in California by the courts for capital murder, they go to death row at San Quentin. It's located above the five tiers of cells in north block. Only north block has a sixth floor. Trust me, you do not want to be housed there. Everyone housed there has been condemned to die, and all are considered as *dead men walking*. At least so it was at the time I was there. I've been told the guards now shout, "Escort!" Saying "Dead man walking" wasn't politically correct.

The only reason for a death row inmate to come down off death row was for things such as a doctor's appointment, dentist appointment, attorney visit, etc. At no time were they permitted to mingle with the general population. So when they were being escorted to these various appointments, the guard would shout out, "Dead man walking!" That meant for you to clear a path and stand clear of the guards and condemned man walking.

It seemed to me that every time they brought a death row inmate out, the guards escorting him were big dudes. There would be one guard on either side of the condemned prisoner. They didn't pick the small guards to escort these guys. When they shouted, it was with authority and meaning! They weren't playing around. They wanted a path cleared and cleared now! It was quite an experience the first few times I saw it.

To see these death row inmates being escorted with the guards really made you think. You looked at them and couldn't help but feel compassion for them. At least I couldn't. You didn't know the crime they committed, but you being a prisoner as well couldn't help but feel sorry for them. Maybe it wasn't even that but something deeper.

Let me ask you, what crime is deserving of death? I suppose it depends on whom you ask. One may say, "murder," while the other will say, "child molestation." Rape might be another's. I want you to stop and really think about this: How big or how small does a crime have to be in order for it to be worthy of death? I know I used to have my opinion on the matter, and I'm sure everyone does, but what is yours?

I believe there is only One with the authority to determine what crime is deserving of death, and that is God. The obvious crimes deserving of death are recorded in the Bible known as the Ten Commandments, but are they limited to those? All crimes are worthy of death according to God's standard, and He states that: "For the wages of sin is death" (Romans 6:23).

I want to quote just a few verses out of the Bible to give you an idea of God's perspective: "And he who strikes his father or his mother shall surely be put to death. He who kidnaps a man and sells him, or if he is found in his hand, shall surely be put to death. And he who curses his father or his mother shall surely be put to death" (Exodus 21:15–17). "But the cowardly, unbelieving, abominable, murderers, sexually immoral, sorcerers, idolaters, and all liars shall have their part in the lake which burns with fire and brimstone, which is the second death" (Revelation 21:8).

God is Holy and cannot condone any type of sin or crime. His standard is perfection, and Jesus says in Matthew 5:48, "Therefore you shall be perfect, just as your Father in heaven is perfect." There are no big or small crimes! The Bible takes it even a step further and says, "For whoever shall keep the whole law, and yet stumble in one point, he is guilty of all" (James 2:10).

I can't count how many crimes I've committed in the verses quoted above. How about you? You ever tell a lie? Dead man walking! How about cursing your father or mother? Dead man walking! I guess I could go on and on, but I think you get the point. Like the apostle James said, if you broke one law, then in God's eyes you broke them all, and that makes you a dead man walking.

That's why I still see dead men and women walking to this day. Everyone has sins that they have committed, which God has to punish. God says in His Word, "The soul who sins shall die" (Ezekiel 18:20). If we are honest with ourselves, we will all admit that at one time or another in our life, we have committed sin. Believe it or not, I have run across some that say they don't or haven't. All that I can say to that is, you're telling a lie right now.

Did you know even your thoughts can be sin? Jesus said, "But I say to you that whoever looks at a woman to lust for her has already committed adultery with her in his heart" (Matthew 5:28). Come on, men; let's keep it real. How many times have we done that? Now I know women don't have that problem. (Yeah right!) We all are sinners and are dead men or women walking.

The Bible teaches that there is a book in heaven that records every sin every person has ever committed. That should be an eye-opener in and of itself. How thick is each one of our books? That isn't even the question; one sin is a death sentence.

It would be like putting one drop of poison in a glass of water and me giving it to you to drink. Would you drink it? Of course not! It is kind of like that with God. One sin contaminates us, and God can have nothing to do with sin. In fact, He has to punish that sin. He loves us and doesn't want to punish us, but because He is a just judge (Psalm 7:11), He has to pronounce judgment on sin.

When I went to superior court in Glenn County for taking that gun away from the highway patrolman, I knew the judge I went in front of surely wasn't going to let me go. Being a just judge, he couldn't! Believe me when I say God's standard is a lot higher than any human judge's standard. So why should we expect God to be any less of a just judge than a superior court judge?

Let me pose this question to you: If you were on death row at San Quentin State Prison and someone were to say to you, "I can get you off death row," would you say, "No thanks, I want to stay and die one day." Or would you say, "How can I get out of this death sentence?"

There is such a person that can take you off San Quentin's death row. That would be the governor of the state of California. He can commute that person's death sentence into a life sentence. If the governor chooses to, he can pardon your crime, and you would be taken off death row. It's that simple!

But if the governor took a person off death row, or let's say many people off death row just because he chose to, would he be right in doing so? I think the people of the state of California would be demanding the governor's head for letting these condemned men or women go.

It's a sobering thought, but we are all sentenced to die. We may not be physically on death row at San Quentin, but we are all sentenced to death. How do I know this? Because we all die someday!

So that makes us all dead men walking. People do not want to hear that they are condemned to die. God is right in punishing sin, and I think most will agree with that. If we don't agree with that, then why did we institute laws into our society? The law is twofold: It is in place to deter people from breaking it, and to punish those who are.

So the law says we must punish crime, and God agrees. After all, He is the one who made the law. So if God has to punish sin, how do we get out of this death sentence? How can God let the guilty go free? He can't, but He did make a way off death row.

CHAPTER FOURTEEN

Good News

THE GOOD NEWS IS THAT it is through God's Son, Jesus Christ, that we may be saved from the eternal death sentence we all have. Jesus said, "For God did not send His Son into the world to condemn the world, but that the world through Him might be saved" (John 3:17).

It is by grace we are saved, and the word *grace* just means "*unmerited favor.*" We can't earn, nor do we deserve to go to heaven. We are all guilty of sin and rightly deserving of judgment. But God made a way for us to be saved from eternal death. The Bible says, "For by grace you have been saved, through faith and that not of yourselves. It is the gift of God, not of works lest anyone should boast" (Ephesians 2:8–9).

To better understand what grace is, let me give you an example. It's like when a Boy Scout or Girl Scout does some sort of task to earn a merit badge. A Boy Scout may earn a merit badge for backpacking, fire safety, etc. That child made the effort to learn the task at hand, performed it, and received a merit badge for completing it. *It is not like that with God.* We can't earn God's favor. Can we do things that please God? Of course, but those things will not save us from eternal death.

Heaven is a free gift, as the verse in Ephesians says, "the gift of God." Because it's a gift, you can't earn it, nor do you work for it. If I were to give you a birthday present and you received it, what did you do to earn or deserve it? Nothing. You just took it! What if I gave you that gift then sent you a bill for it? Would it still be a gift? Of course not! Receiving eternal life is that simple. You just receive the gift that God so freely offers to whosoever will take it.

Heaven has to be a free gift because of the nature of man. The Bible says, "For all have sinned and fall short of the glory of God" (Romans 6:23). If I were to ask you what sin is, how would you answer that? Some people have trouble answering that question, but the Bible defines *sin* as "missing the mark."

I touched on this in the previous chapter, but sin is a serious subject, and it is one that we really need to understand. God says that even our thoughts can be sin. We talked about murder being a sin, but Jesus says, "Whoever is angry with his brother without a cause shall be in danger of the judgment" (Mathew 5:22). In other words, you've committed murder in your heart.

Here is another example of sin in the book of James: "Therefore, to him who knows to do good, and does not do it, to him it is sin" (James 4:17).

With those examples in mind, how many times do we sin in a day? How many bad thoughts do we have in a day? How many times in a day do we see someone who needs our help and not help when we should or could? Or what about when someone cuts us off in traffic and we have a few choice words or thoughts of them? *The list can go on and on.*

That's why heaven has to be a free gift. We are sinners deserving the judgment of God. Remember God's standard to get into heaven? Perfection! I quoted the verse from Matthew 5:48 earlier about being perfect as your Father in heaven is perfect. In context, it is talking about perfect love. Love your enemies, bless those who curse you, etc. I'm not perfect, nor do I know anyone that is. Do you see the dilemma we are in? We have to have a perfect love for others to get into heaven, yet none have that perfection.

The Bible teaches that God is love (1 John 4:8). It also teaches that God is a just judge (Psalm 7:11). God loves us and does not want to punish us, but being a just judge, He has to. If God didn't punish our sin, would He be a just judge? No, He wouldn't!

God, knowing we couldn't save ourselves based on our own merits, sent His Son into the world to resolve our problem. It really wasn't God's problem; we're the ones who chose to sin, yet God made it His problem: "But God so loved the world that He gave His only begotten Son, that whoever believes in Him should not perish but have everlasting life" (John 3:16). "*Not perish*"—you see that? God does not want us on death row any more than we want to be there. In fact, God says, "For I have no pleasure in the death of one who dies, says the Lord God. Therefore turn and live" (Ezekiel 18:32).

Jesus is an interesting person, and finding out who He is and what He has done for me changed my life. Who is Jesus to you? There are several names or titles for who He is: "The Lamb of God" (John 1:29), "I am the bread of life" (John 6:48). Another one of His names is the Word (John 1:1)—"In the beginning was the Word, and the Word was with God and the Word was God." Then if you drop down to verse 14 of the same chapter, it says, "The Word became flesh and dwelt among us."

So every time you see the word *Word*, you could insert Jesus's name in there. So He was fully man and fully God. Jesus was from the beginning and was with God and was God, and He became flesh in the form of a human at birth.

Jesus' birth differs from ours in the sense that His Father was God. God the Father is without sin; Jesus having the same nature as His Father; Righteous, Co-Eternal, Co-Existent, Co-Equal, etc., makes Him sinless as well. He became a Man through the virgin birth of Mary, and the life He lived here on earth was sinless. Was He tempted to sin during that time? You better believe it! He didn't give into the desires of the flesh as we do with the sin nature we have. Jesus was, is, and always will be perfect. He is the perfection we need to get us into heaven. As quoted earlier, "be perfect as my Father in heaven is perfect" (Matthew 5:48).

So that's who Jesus is! What He has done for us is purchase a place in heaven. Condition: It is only for those who *trust and believe* in what He did for them. Jesus said, "In my Father's house are many mansions; if it were not so, I would have told you. I go to prepare a place for you. And if I go and prepare a place for you, I will come again and receive you to My-self, that where I am, there you may be also" (John 14:2–3).

In 2 Corinthians 5:21, it says, "For He [God, the Father)] made Him [God, the Son] who knew no sin to be sin for us, that we might become the righteousness of God in Him." Since Jesus was without sin, He was not deserving of any punishment. He took on our sins upon Himself to pay the price we couldn't pay.

CHAPTER FIFTEEN

Paid in Full

THERE IS A BOOK IN heaven that records every one of our sins. We all have a book, and everyone will be judged according to what is written in their book. I'm sure some books are thicker than others, but as mentioned before, how thick your book is isn't the point.

The person that has one sin recorded in their book, and the person who has seventy thousand sins recorded in theirs, are both going to be condemned: "The wages of *sin* is death" (Romans 6:23, emphasis added). It doesn't say *sins*; it says *sin*! One sin will separate you from God and heaven.

Do you see why we can't save ourselves? When Jesus was on the cross being crucified for our sins and was about die, He cried out a word which in the Greek language is *tetelestai*. In the English language, it can be translated as *finished, complete, paid*, etc.

Back in the day when Jesus walked this earth, it was an accounting term. When someone bought something, they would stamp on it: *tetelestai* (paid). That is what Jesus did. He paid for the sins that are written in our book: "And I saw the dead, small and great, standing before God, and books were opened. And another book was opened; which is the Book of Life. And the dead were judged according to their works, by the things which were written in the books. The sea gave up the dead who were in it, and Death and Hades delivered up the dead who were in them. And they were judged, each one according to his works. Then Death and Hades were cast into the lake of fire. This is the second death. And anyone not found written in the Book of Life was cast into the lake of fire" (Revelation 20:12–15).

There are books in heaven, and if anyone thinks they can get to heaven based on their own merits, they are in for a big surprise. Notice there is our book of sins and there is a book of life. Jesus is the only way to get your name written in the Book of Life.

God's Word is true, whether you believe it or not. And that is the most important question you'll ever have to ask yourself, do I believe it? If not, then the Word of God says you will be judged according to your works. Are you confident in your works? Are you really a good person? Are you perfect? If you are, then you have nothing to worry about. But if not, then call on the name of Jesus so that He can write your name in the Book of Life.

We are deserving of His judgment, and unless we believe Jesus paid for the sins that are written in our book, we will experience that second death, which is eternal. Do you want to spend eternity with God in heaven or with Satan in hell?

There is only one way to get to heaven. That is by faith! Everyone has faith, but the question is this: What are you putting yours in? Is it because you're a good person or because you help feed the poor? Or is it because you go to church? Possibly it's because you know there is a god. James 2:19 says, "You believe that there is one God. You do well. Even the demons believe and tremble."

You can believe there is a god, but that will not save you from having your sins judged. You can go to church. You can feed the poor. You can do all sorts of good things, but that will not save you from Judgment Day. You can be perfect from this day forward, but what about the sins you've already committed? They have to be paid for.

Look at it this way. Suppose you're in the river that leads to the Niagara Falls. You've been staying afloat for a long time out there, but now you're starting to drown. All of a sudden, a log comes floating by, and you grab hold of it. *Oh boy, I'm safe!* But what happens when you get to the end of the river and come to the falls? You are no longer safe but go over and are killed.

But suppose before you come to the falls, you see Jesus on the bank of the river. He throws you a rope and says, "*Grab the rope. I'll pull you to safety.*" What do you have to do to be saved? Most people say, "Grab the rope." That would be correct, but before you can grab the rope, you first have to let go of the log. That log represents what your trusting in to save you: "I'm a good person," "I go to church," "I feed the poor," etc.

Quit trusting in something you *think* will save you! We're going down this river of life thinking we're good people and we're going to heaven based on what we've done. Don't fall for the lie! Satan wants us to believe we can save ourselves. The truth is, we are on our way to hell apart from Christ.

Think about that; when we say, "*I'm* a good person," or "*I* go to church," or "*I* feed the poor." Who is it your trusting in? It's *I*. I can't save myself no matter how good I am because I am a sinner. It is those sins that caused me to have a death sentence.

Does God want us to do good things? Of course He does! But don't trust in the things you do to get you off death row. I knew guys that had been on death row but were taken off when the California Supreme Court ruled/deemed the death penalty to be cruel and unusual punishment, thereby abolishing the death penalty. Of course the death penalty has since been reinstated.

There was this guy we used to call Old Man Modesto who was on death row for killing two people. At that time, I think he had been incarcerated for over forty years. He was one of the nicest people I had ever met. This guy would take his shirt off his back and give it to you.

Can people who have committed such heinous crimes still do good things? Of course! But because he is now a nice guy, does that mean he shouldn't be held accountable for his crimes? No! No more than we should get off just because we do good things.

"For we are His [God's] workmanship, created in Christ Jesus for good works, which God prepared beforehand that we should walk in them" (Ephesians 2:10). God created us to do good things, but the Bible also says, "For it is God who works in you both to will and do for His good pleasure" (Philippians 2:13). So any good you do is for the glory of God because He is the one working it in and then out of you.

Evil people can do good things without the Spirit of God in them. But as the verse just quoted says, it is God who makes us do the good things. I believe that's why even bad people can do good things.

CHAPTER SIXTEEN

Turn and Live

THERE IS A WORD IN the Bible and it's meaning is crucial to know and understand. That word is *repent*. Maybe you have heard someone use this word before, but do you know what it means? *Repent* means "change of mind," or "to turn." One thing we need to change our mind about is thinking our good works can save us.

Once we have come to terms with who Jesus is, we need to trust in what it was He did for us on the cross: "For I delivered to you first of all that which I also received that Christ died for our sins according to the Scriptures, and that He was buried, and that He rose again the third day according to the Scriptures" (1 Corinthians 15:3–4). He died for us, and what I like best is that He has risen from the dead. Jesus died so that we may live. *Do you believe this?*

Did you know that there are different types of faith? The type of faith we need is not a temporal faith. Temporal faith looks kind of like this: We pray and ask God to heal us of a sickness. Or we ask for help with our financial needs. Maybe we ask Him to provide food and clothing. It's alright to pray for those things, but that type of faith is temporal. Once our prayers are answered; we go back to our lives forgetting all about what God did. That is until we need Him again. God is not like a spare tire we keep in the trunk of our car and pull Him out when we need Him. He wants us to call on Him for all of life's problems, circumstances and situations. Not just for the things He already knows we need. Most importantly: Call on Him for the forgiveness of your sins, and the salvation of your soul.

We talked about it not being just an intellectual faith. You can know there is a god, but that won't save you either. It would be like me going to the White House and telling the guard to let me in because I know who President Trump is. Do you think they would let me in? Of course not, I might know who Trump is, but Trump doesn't know me. Unlike President Trump, God does know who we are, but we need to know who God's Son is.

There is something else I want to say about the word *repent*. I mentioned that it means "change of mind" or "to turn." But turn from what? Sin! Christians are not perfect, just forgiven. So when we do sin, which we will, we ask God to forgive us. God's Word says, "If we confess our sins, He is faithful and just to forgive us our sins and to cleanse us from all unrighteousness" (1 John 1:9).

With that being said, if and when we sin, we need to be willing to turn from it and turn to God and ask Him to forgive us.

If you're not familiar with the I-5 Interstate Highway here in Orange County, California, it runs north and south. If you want to go to Mexico, you need to be going south. Now suppose you were heading north in the direction of Los Angeles. What would you have to do to get to Mexico? Obviously, get off the freeway, make a U-turn, and start going south in the right direction.

It is kind of like that when we fall into sin. We are heading in the wrong direction. We need to get off that road to destruction and turn around and head toward God. We repent and turn from our sin and ask Him to forgive us. It really is that simple.

Today has to be the day of your salvation. I say *today* because you're not promised tomorrow. On September 11, 2001, in New York, everyone was going about their daily routine. Do you think those people that went to work in the World Trade Center thought that would be their last day of life? I don't think they did either. If they had known, I'm sure they would have done something to prevent it. If you knew you would spend eternity in hell, wouldn't you do something about it? You can!

This is a simple prayer you can pray to God: "Dear Heavenly Father, thank you that it is by grace I can be saved, that my salvation isn't based on what I can do for You but only based on what You did for me. Thank you for sending Your Son, Jesus, to die on the cross for me and paying the price I couldn't pay. I put my trust and faith in Your Son, Jesus, alone for my salvation. Forgive me of my sins and be my Lord and Savior. Thank you for raising Your Son from the grave and giving me life in and through Him. In Jesus's name, I pray. Amen!"

If you were sincere in that prayer to God, the Bible teaches that you have been born again. Obviously, we can't go back into our mother's womb and be born again physically. This birth is from God and is a spiritual birth. The Spirit of God came into you the moment you prayed that prayer, and His Spirit in you is the new birth. You no longer live according to the desires of your body but by the Spirit of God in you. It is a life I wouldn't trade for the world.

God's promise is that you will never perish but have everlasting life. *He has a place in heaven waiting for you.* Romans 10:9 says, "If you confess with your mouth the Lord Jesus, and believe in your heart that God raised Him from the dead, you will be saved." That is God's promise to you, and His promises are yes!

CHAPTER SEVENTEEN

Lord of My Life

IF YOU PRAYED FOR GOD to forgive you of your sins and asked him to come into your life, that makes Jesus your Savior. Thank God He is our Savior, but He also needs to be our Lord. The verse in the previous chapter said, "Confess with your mouth the *Lord* Jesus." *Lord* means "master," and if He is the master, that makes us the servants. We are no longer our own but have been purchased with a price, and that price was paid by Jesus's blood: "For you were bought at a price; therefore glorify God in your body and in your spirit which are God's" (1 Corinthians 6:20). We belong to Jesus now! He is the one in whom we trust to get us through this life and into eternity.

Since Jesus has been Lord of my life, life has not always been a walk in the park. God didn't say it would be. I had trouble before coming to Christ, and I still do. I run into trials, tribulations, and temptations, but it's different now; God is with me and gets me through it all.

I heard a message the other day that really got me to think. When we take our eyes off Jesus, that's when we usually get offtrack. Jennie Lusko made this profound statement: She said she would tell this to her Sunday School kids to get their attention. "One, two, three, eyes on me." Then the kids were to reply, "One, two, eyes on you."

Then she referenced Psalms 123:1–2, which says, "Unto You I lift up my eyes, O' You who dwell in the heavens. Behold, as the eyes of servants look to the hand of their masters, as the eyes of the maid to the hand of her mistress, so our eyes look to the Lord our God, until He has mercy on us." The inference is: God is saying to us, "One, two, three, eyes on me." And we're to respond; "one, two, eyes on you." We need to keep our eyes on Jesus. It keeps us from focusing on the not-so-good things in life.

My mom passed away last year, with my sister dying three weeks later. It was a difficult time. If I didn't have God with me to get me through it, I might have used that as a reason to go back to drugs. God doesn't take us out of the trials in life, but He does get us through them.

In the past, I *probably* would have turned back to shooting drugs with that tragedy happening. But my Lord and Savior Jesus Christ had a better solution. He entrusted me with overseeing the evangelism ministry we have (previously mentioned).

The good news in the passing of my mom and sister is that I got to tell them about Jesus and the free gift of eternal life. They both received that gift by simply asking God to forgive them and to be their Lord and Savior. I will see them again, and I can rejoice in that promise from God.

Have you ever been to a funeral and heard people talk about the person that has died? I don't know how many times I've heard it said: "They're in a better place." That is not necessarily true! Obviously, we want them to be, but unless they have placed their faith in Jesus, *they are not.*

That offends some people, but it really shouldn't. God provided a way to be in a better place. You just have to ask Him to forgive you and to save you from going into eternity separated from Him forever. Why some people don't want to do that, I really can't understand. The truth is, some don't and won't. *It breaks my heart.* God gave us free will, and God allows us to make our own decision. The choice is ours! We can choose life, or we can choose death, but there are consequences to both.

It's been just a little over eight years now that I have been out of prison. I am so blessed and so happy even when I'm not. Kind of an oxymoronic statement, but I know the God I serve and the promise that He is always with me. He gets me through thick and thin and is the one I can count on in all situations. He is the Lord of my life!

CHAPTER EIGHTEEN

What if I Died Today?

OVER THE PERIOD OF MY lifetime, I have been close to death on more than one occasion. I ask myself from time to time, what if I died one of those times? Every time I've had one of those close encounters with death is when I didn't have Jesus as my Lord and Savior. I would have spent eternity in hell. It gives me the creeps thinking about that.

When I was strung out like a dog on heroin, I had a near-death experience I will never forget. One reason being, I still have the scars to remind me of it. This happened when I was constantly injecting needles into my veins. Over a long period of time, my veins started to collapse from the abuse of drugs.

For years, I used only my arms to shoot drugs, moving from one vein to another. I used my neck for a while, but it was too hard to look into a mirror and direct the needle into the juggler. After destroying all the veins in my arms, I went to using the veins in my legs. After years of doing this, the veins in my legs started to disappear. I can't explain it, but I'm sure there is a medical term for what was about to take place.

The injection site on both of my lower extremities became large open wounds. The medical term for this is called cellulites. I also developed an infection in the bone on both legs. The veins in my legs started to vanish when this thing happened, which I can't explain; I could put a needle anywhere in my leg where the open wound was and get a blood register. A blood register is when you see blood come up into the syringe from pulling back on the plunger. This lets you know you're in the vein. That's why a drug addict gets a rush; because the drugs are going directly into the blood stream. When I injected the dope in my leg, I would get an immediate rush. Of course that caused the wound to become larger and larger. That was because the dope wasn't actually going into the vein. Again, I can't explain it, but because I was getting the rush I desired, I continued in the practice of shooting *anywhere* in the open wound. Death was lying at my door, and I didn't even know it.

It's amazing how your body tells you you're dying. Only a few people knew about my legs and their condition. It wasn't something I advertised. I was told to go to the hospital several times by these friends, but I chose not to listen. Pondering on that, I was choosing death over life by not going to the hospital. It wasn't until *I knew* I was dying that I did.

I started to notice my blood wasn't the normal color. I knew something was wrong. I went to the hospital emergency room, and the attending doctor ordered a complete blood work up. Once the lab person arrived to draw the blood, he couldn't find a vein. He then proceeded to search for an artery to draw from. One thing about getting blood out of an artery is, it hurts! Another thing is, it fills the test tube up in an instant.

I can remember vividly when the lab technician found an artery and the blood filled the tube. I asked him, "What is that?" He said, "It's your blood." It was dark brown in color, and I couldn't believe what I was seeing. It wasn't good.

They immediately admitted me into the hospital and started a regimen of high-powered antibiotics. These antibiotics were so potent, they had to take my blood daily just to make sure they weren't giving me too much. I guess that could have been detrimental to my health as well.

After a few days of medication, the color of my blood started to return to its normal color. It was maybe a week later up in my hospital room that the lab technician that took my blood in the ER came to draw blood. As we were talking, he said, "The amount of infection that was in your blood, you should have been dead." I knew I was dying, and he just confirmed it.

Had I died that day, I would have spent eternity in hell. Looking back on that incident, I know God was with me even in my worst condition. I said before that I believed in God but lived like the devil. God had a plan for my life, and He knew one day I would surrender my will to His and write this book to warn you.

Nobody has to spend eternity in hell. God does not want that for any of His creation. God loves you and me and wants us to be in heaven with Him when we die. Think about this: The little seventy or eighty years we live here on this earth is nothing compared to eternity.

I had a friend describe eternity like this: If you were to take Mount Everest and brush a cloth over it until the mountain disappeared from the continued brushing, that's when eternity begins—in other words, a long time! I don't think the human mind can even comprehend eternity.

I spent seven weeks in the hospital and had to have skin grafted onto both legs. That skin had to come from somewhere, and it came from my upper legs. It wasn't a pleasant thing to experience either. I'm talking about a pain you never forget.

The sad thing is, I used drugs in the same area after getting out of the hospital and lost the skin that was grafted on both legs. It was years later when I got busted and was sentenced to thirteen years that they did another skin graft. Thank God I was incarcerated when they did it. I probably would have repeated my old habits and lost them again.

The entire seven weeks I was in the hospital, I had friends bringing me heroin. With friends like that, who needs enemies, right? Since I had no veins anywhere, the physicians put in a central line. It's a tube that goes into your chest and directly to the heart. I thought that was great! Now I could use the injection port in my line to shoot heroin straight to the heart! What a rush.

That's how terribly bad off I was. It's a trap the devil has so many people caught up in, and they can't see their way out. That is a lie straight from the pit of hell. Jesus is the way out!

Drug addiction is real for so many people today in our society. I believe all drugs are addictive to some degree, but especially heroin. It is so hard to get off because of the physical withdrawals. I would say to the person who is strung out on heroin, "Do what you have to do to get off it. But once you do, you need to seek God." I'm not going to lie; when a person is going through withdrawals, you can't do anything but think of that next fix. For me, God used jail to get me off the drugs. For you, it might be a drug program. For others, it might be a hospital or divine deliverance from God Himself. God can do what He wants, in the way He wants. I thank God for my freedom from drugs, even though it took a thirteen-year sentence to do it.

You can be drug-free, which is great, but that doesn't determine your eternal state. Only you can determine where you will spend eternity. God gives you the choice. It's a matter of faith and whom you place that faith in.

If you were to die today, do you know where you would spend eternity? If you don't know, you can know: "These things are written that you may know you have eternal life" (1 John 5:13). Don't wait until tomorrow. If I had waited to go to the hospital for another day or two or even a week, I don't think I would be here to tell you there is a way to heaven, and that way is through Jesus Christ.

I can tell you story after story of my past, present and future, but the only story you need to know is the story of Jesus. His story is recorded in the Bible, and it is only His story and His sacrifice that can save you. I pray that you read it today, accept it as truth, and trust in it to save you.

CHAPTER NINETEEN

For Christians Only

CHRISTIANS, THIS IS FOR YOU only. Whether you just now gave your life to the Lord Jesus or have been a Christian for years, it's your responsibility to tell someone. "And since we have the same spirit of faith, according to what is written, I believed and therefore I spoke, we also believe and therefore speak, knowing that He who raised up the Lord Jesus will also raise us up with Jesus, and will present us with you" (2 Corinthians 4:13–14).

The statistics are that 95 percent of Christians do not go out and share their faith. It is our commission to do so. If you don't know anything else, except the verse just quoted, you need to tell it to someone.

Fear is one of the obstacles between us and sharing. The acronym for FEAR is *false evidence appearing real.* How many times have we been afraid of something, and that which we feared never came to pass? Say we share and someone rejects the good news. Who is it they are rejecting? Not you, but God. That didn't stop Jesus from sharing the truth, and it shouldn't stop us.

Maybe it's because you feel inadequate. You are! I don't know of anyone that's perfect in sharing God's good news other than Him. But God "hasn't given us a spirit of fear, but of power and of love and of a sound mind" (2 Timothy 1:7). Just as you have trusted Jesus to save you, you have to trust that He will be with you when you are telling someone about Him.

I titled this chapter the way I did for a reason. You wouldn't want other religious groups telling people about who Jesus is, would you? I'm sure their knowledge and understanding of who Jesus is differs from that of a Christian.

That is our problem today. So many people have heard about Jesus, but who is it that told them about Jesus? Is it a cult? Or maybe it's from someone who has never read the Bible? Who is going to tell them about Jesus? *Is it you?*

Whoever it is, that person does need to be *equipped*. We get equipped by reading and studying God's Word. "And He Himself gave some to be apostles, some prophets, some evangelist, and some pastors and teachers, for the *equipping* of the saints for the work of ministry" (Ephesians 4:11–12, emphasis added). We get equipped in the church. I would urge you to get involved and equipped. You won't regret it!

Don't let the lack of knowledge stop you from doing what God has called you to do. Especially when everything we need is right in the pages of scripture. When we were in school as children, the teacher was there to teach. In church, the pastor is there to teach. If you don't know how to share your faith, ultimately the blame falls on you. I would ask the question, Are you trusting in God to be with you and to empower you or not? His Word says He will! *Do you believe this?*

Our belief as born-again believers in Jesus Christ is just what the Bible says, "I am the way, the truth, and the life. No one comes to the Father except through me" (John 14:6). Jesus is the only way to heaven for the simple reason that He's the only one who died and rose from the grave. No other religions make that claim, nor can they. Only Jesus has done that! Our hope is in the resurrected Christ!

We all have relatives, friends, coworkers, and neighbors. How many of them would you like to see go to hell? Don't answer that! I would hope none, since we know God doesn't want any to go there. Our heart needs to be for the lost. We were once lost until someone told us about Jesus. Aren't you thankful for the person who did tell you about Jesus? Return that favor by sharing Jesus with someone else. You might be the only person preventing someone from going into eternity without Jesus.

I had many sleepless nights because I didn't know the eternal state of my dad. When I think about how little I shared with him about Jesus, it saddens my heart. I could have said more! I didn't miss that opportunity with my mom and sister. I learned how to share my faith and made sure they understood what it meant to be saved. Thank God they received the gift and accepted Jesus as Lord of their life. As previously mentioned, I will see them in heaven. What a blessing it is to know that!

Even though we share our faith, it doesn't mean it will be received. We can't save anyone anyway; that's up to God. But God has given us a treasure: "But we have this treasure in earthen vessels that the excellence of the power may be of God and not of us" (2 Corinthians 4:7). That vessel is us, and the treasure is the Gospel. So we have the good news (treasure) in us to share with the world. But look at the verse again: *"The power may be of God and not of us."* It is God who is the source of our power to share. Rest on Him!

When Jesus gave us the great commission to go out and tell people about Him and to baptize them, He said something very encouraging to me: "Teaching them to observe all things that I have commanded you; and lo, *I am with you always*, even to the end of the age" (Matthew 28:20, emphasis added). To know God is with us when we are sharing our faith is quite comforting to me.

I can't do it on my own, and if I did, it wouldn't amount to much anyways. We need His Spirit to be with us and give us the words to speak. "But the Helper, the Holy Spirit, whom the Father will send in My name, He will teach you all things, and bring to your remembrance all things that I said to you" (John 14:26). The thing about that verse is, you can't remember something you never knew. Once you know God's Word, then His promise to you is that He will remind you of what He said when you need it the most.

The Lord wants to bless you and others. He blesses others by using you to share the treasure that is within you with them. Then in turn, you're blessed because you possibly planted a seed, watered it, or better yet, harvested the fruit. It says in (1 Corinthians 3:7): "So then neither he who plants is anything, nor he who waters, but God who gives the increase." All glory to God!

Angels in heaven rejoice every time a sinner repents and gives their life to God. I have personally experienced that joy the angels have, and it's awesome. I want you Christians to experience it for yourselves.

I hope and pray this book has blessed and encouraged someone to draw closer to God and to surrender their life completely to Him. The Lord loves you and wants to save you. *I pray that you let Him.*

CPSIA information can be obtained
at www.ICGtesting.com
Printed in the USA
LVHW090311240520
656341LV00004BA/493